Intergenerational Cell Resources

five series of meeting outlines
for the intergenerational cell

Daphne Kirk

This edition published in 1999 by
KEVIN MAYHEW LTD
Buxhall
Stowmarket
Suffolk IP14 3DJ

© 1999 Daphne Kirk

The right of Daphne Kirk to be identified as the author
of this work has been asserted by her in accordance
with the Copyright, Designs and Patents Act 1988.

Material in this book is copyright-free provided that
it is used for the purpose for which the book is intended
within the individual cell group. Reproduction of any of the
contents of this book for commercial purposes is subject
to the usual copyright restrictions.

All rights reserved.

Scripture references are taken from the Holy Bible, New International Version,
unless otherwise stated. Copyright © 1973, 1978, 1984, by International
Bible Society. Used by permission of Hodder & Stoughton Limited.

0 1 2 3 4 5 6 7 8 9

ISBN 1 84003 381 9
Catalogue No 1500279

Cover design by Jaquetta Sergeant
Edited by Helen Elliot
Typesetting by Louise Selfe
Printed and bound in Great Britain

Contents

ABOUT THIS BOOK	5
INTRODUCTION	7
Structure of the cell meeting	7
Kids' slot	12
Tips for intergenerational cell leaders	14
Structure of the meeting outlines	16
THE PRAYER MEETING	19
THE SOCIAL OUTREACH MEETING	21
SERIES ONE: THE LORD'S SUPPER	22
Week 1	22
Kids' Slot material	26
Week 2	27
Kids' Slot material	30
Week 3	31
Kids' Slot material	33
Week 4	34
Kids' Slot material	36
Delegation forms	37
SERIES TWO: PRAYER	47
Week 1	47
Kids' Slot material	51
Week 2	52
Kids' Slot material	55
Week 3	56
Kids' Slot material	60
Week 4	61
Kids' Slot material	63
Delegation forms	65
SERIES THREE: WHO WILL BE A SERVANT?	74
Week 1	74
Kids' Slot material	77
Week 2	78
Kids' Slot material	80
Week 3	81
Kids' Slot material	83
Week 4	84
Kids' Slot material	86
Delegation forms	87

SERIES FOUR: RELATIONSHIPS, BASED ON THE BOOK OF RUTH	96
Week 1	98
Kids' Slot material	101
Week 2	103
Kids' Slot material	106
Week 3	108
Kids' Slot material	111
Week 4	112
Kids' Slot material	115
Delegation forms	117
SERIES FIVE: EXTRACTS FROM 1 TIMOTHY	125
Week 1	126
Kids' Slot material	130
Week 2	132
Kids' Slot material	135
Week 3	136
Kids' Slot material	138
Week 4	139
Kids' Slot material	141
Delegation forms	143
APPENDIX 1: SEMINARS	153
APPENDIX 2: OTHER INTERGENERATIONAL CELL MATERIAL FROM DAPHNE KIRK	154
APPENDIX 3: USEFUL FORMS . . .	155

About this book

This book is intended to supplement *Heirs Together*, where the principles and practice of intergenerational Cell Church are clearly set out. Without these, the content of this book will lose much of its power. These meeting outlines are offered as tools for the facilitating of the cell meeting, but you will need to allow the Holy Spirit to permeate them to give them power and life.

Remember that, unless otherwise stated, everything mentioned is for adults, young people and children. The word 'everyone' means 'adults, young people and children'. The word 'group' means 'adults, young people and children'! The word 'members' means 'adults, young people and children'! The word 'all' means 'adults, young people and children'! This may seem to be labouring the point, but too often those words are interpreted as meaning 'adults', particularly when they are read in Scripture, or in a church context.

*For all cell leaders –
to whom this book is prayerfully dedicated*

Introduction

Structure of the cell meeting

Outline

Jesus is always the centre of the meeting, and in Him lives are changed and relationships are formed. From this secure base the group (adults, young people and children) reach out to the lost. The cell meeting is where the community comes together. It is a part of the lifestyle created between adults, young people and children who are becoming increasingly vulnerable and open with each other.

The four 'Ws' form the skeleton of the meeting:

Welcome, which includes the icebreaker
Worship, which includes the offering
Word, which may include ministry
Witness

The meeting should last no more than two hours from start to finish. Never go beyond that time. Initially more time will be spent on the Welcome when a new group forms, then more time in the Worship and Word, until later, as the cell prepares for multiplication, more emphasis is placed on the Witness. However, all the components need to be present throughout the cycle.

Some groups find it more beneficial to let the Witness flow out of the Worship. This may be (a) because the Witness section is often the hardest one, or (b) to allow for ministry to flow at the end of the meeting.

Leaders

The cell meeting may seem very structured, but there are important reasons why this is so. Leaders are raised in every cell, so that multiplication can take place swiftly and effectively. The model allows the cell meeting to be reproduced by most people. The meeting is a place where gifts can emerge and be nurtured in adults and children. Its simple structure allows everyone to feel secure and able to lead at least a part of it, and helps the group to develop within the values of cell: 'love God, love each other, love the lost.' All leaders have their own strengths and weaknesses; someone with a preference for evangelism will spend longer on witness, another might prefer longer in worship, while another might prefer to spend more time in prayer. The basic structure ensures that everyone receives a 'balanced diet'.

The effectiveness of the four 'Ws' will be seen in the way that the cell leader internalises the material and therefore delivers it within the flow of the Holy Spirit. Each section is given as part of a skeleton, which each group will clothe with their own character. Cells who have been given exactly the same material will each produce a new anointing and a fresh identity. Like the human skeleton, the four 'Ws' give shape and support, yet result in each cell meeting having its own identity.

The meeting is primarily designed for edifying and discipling Christians. Friendship evangelism ensures that non-Christians will only be invited when they are ready, and when the group has gone through their two inevitable and necessary early stages of development: the initial honeymoon stage and the period of conflict, before community prepares them for outreach, leading to the celebration of multiplication. Through friendship, non-Christians will have had the opportunity of meeting the group in social settings, so when they attend the meeting, they will encounter a group of friends, and a God they have already been introduced to.

Welcome

This happens when the group first arrives at the home where the meeting is being hosted; each home may be visited in turn. A drink can be offered as people chat informally. Be careful that there is no segregation at this time. Children should be encouraged not to run around the host home, or disappear off to play together. It is their time to chat with and get to know other people, and for others to get to know them. Be sure to put their names on the hosting schedule on a separate occasion from their parents – they love to open the door, serve drinks and feel it is *their* night.

The meeting opens with the icebreaker. This is a time of sharing, so that everyone is involved from the very beginning of the meeting. One person is responsible for bringing a question. The questions can be fun, casual, or informative. They are not designed for intimate sharing, but to allow each person to speak, thus breaking the 'sound barrier'! For example:
- If you could be any part of a car what would you be, and why?
- What was the best thing that happened to you this week?
- If you could meet any historical person who would it be, and why?
- If you were invisible where would you go, and why?
- If you could win one person to Jesus tomorrow, who would it be, and why?

The question is asked by the adult or child responsible for bringing it, then that person answers it first. (This models the time to be spent and gives the flavour of the answers.) The question is then passed around the group in rotation. Children love to take part, and to be responsible for this. Always check the icebreaker question with them before the meeting, to ensure that they have chosen wisely. They may not realise that some questions might be inappropriate and open a 'can of worms'! In the early stages of cell development the icebreaker may last longer and be more interactive than is necessary later.

Worship

This is when we focus on the fact that Jesus is at the very centre of everything we do. Although it is brief, it is the time to welcome the Holy Spirit, and recognise our dependence on Him. Be creative! Singing songs is only one way to worship. If that is the only way we do it, then the perceived message is that only singers can lead this time. Our aim should be that everyone can lead, so, for example:

- read a psalm, or create one together
- bring different items, hand them round, and ask people if they remind them of anything they can thank God for
- take a tape, listen to a song and then join in praising God, as the song has ministered to us
- sing responsively
- encourage people onto their feet
- place a candle in the middle of the room and ask the group what that reminds them of, letting their answers lead into worship
- let each member look out of the window and say what they saw to thank God for
- allow each person to say a simple prayer of thanks
- encourage kneeling, holding hands, speaking to each other, confessing
- use a guitar, tape or sing unaccompanied. Choose songs that are well known and easily repeated

During this time be aware that the Holy Spirit may want to minister through words of knowledge or prophecy (through any age group). Some children will feel more capable of leading this section than others, but the same is true of adults! It may be that a child is paired with someone who is more confident and they work together. Creativity and activity are wonderful in worship. Often it is the children who will lead the adults out of their armchairs! Experience suggests that groups with children generally have more life and creativity in their worship than those without. Everyone enters into it freshly each time. Do not sing 'children's' songs. Sing songs that minister to everyone, i.e. those that have simple words, a catchy tune, and not too many verses. This will also help the adults, and newcomers to the group.

The offering is a part of worship, so it should flow easily during that time. Again, creativity keeps the joy, faith and vibrancy

in giving. Introduce the offering in a variety of ways, for example:
- a testimony of God's faithfulness
- a Scripture story of God's faithfulness
- an article from a Christian magazine

Encourage the person responsible for the offering to bring their own container. This may be something that is special to them, or something they have made specially for this time.

Children often have more faith for finances than adults, and their simple words of exhortation can break spiritual strongholds over this area. Beware! They may bring the most 'creative' offering containers!

Word

This section focuses on applying the Word of God to our own lives. It is *not* an academic Bible study! Led by the Holy Spirit, the cell leader will facilitate discussion relevant to the lives and situations of those present, using questions such as:
- How did that make you feel?
- What would our group look like if we all lived that Scripture?
- What changes would do we need to make in our lives if we are going to live that Scripture?
- What do you think God is saying to us?

If the Word of God is constantly being applied to each person's life within a group where there is trust and openness, then there is no person of whatever age, who cannot take part. If you have an intergenerational celebration, then perhaps the group could share how the message spoke to them (see forms on pages 160 and 161 of Appendix 3. These forms are used in our own celebration and are completed by adults, youth and children and taken to the cell meeting as reminders. They also help everyone to focus during the message.) This section is not usually delegated as skills are needed to draw everyone out, to prevent domination by any one member, and to keep the group focused on the application of the Word. Usually the cell leader will facilitate it, or perhaps the cell leader in training.

We have found children very responsive, and certainly very challenging, in this part of the meeting. As the group honours their input so they will be more confident in sharing (as with adults! – see *Heirs Together*, page 31) The simplicity of applying the Word of God to our lives is for everyone. It becomes relevant to child and adult alike. N.B. It is important to read a version of the Bible that the children will understand (but then most of the adults will understand better, and so will new believers).

Ministry may be appropriate at any time during the meeting. Children will automatically enter into ministry once they know that they are actually needed and welcome in that situation. Once adults release the children to express their faith and operate in the gifts of the Spirit, a new dynamic is released in the meeting, free from religious constraints and preconceived ideas. A key to that release in ministry is that *everyone* (adults and children) gives, and *everyone* receives.

Witness

This begins with a vision statement that creates a focus for the cell, maintaining its vision for reaching the lost. The vision for your Church or your cell could be included at this time.

In this section we focus on the world in which we live; on those around us who need Jesus. Each week the group may
- share how they are getting on with their friends
- send a couple out to prayer walk the street where the meeting is taking place
- plan social events to which they can invite their unsaved friends
- pray for group members who are meeting resistance in their friends
- plan to help each other by building friendships with one another's friends
- pray for 'harvest events' (these are larger gatherings to which the unsaved may be invited, such as seasonal events, drama productions, parties, dinners, bands or concerts).

It is a time when everyone can share their personal problems and the challenges that face them as they reach out to the lost around them. Cell leaders often report that they find this section the hardest to facilitate, which should not surprise us, since the enemy would want this section played down, if not omitted. Creativity helps to keep it alive and prayer pulls down strongholds, but putting the Witness after the Worship can also change the spiritual atmosphere into which the witness section flows.

Children are more spontaneous in their evangelism than we are, but today they face the same disappointments that we do. They need us to empower them. We can plan children's parties to which they can invite their friends. We can reach families if we take our children with us when visiting people's homes. Children love to prayer walk. They will take an interest in your friends if you include them in your prayers and conversations. The intergenerational cell provides a unique opportunity for outreach. As children reach out to their friends, there is a whole network of support and prayer that will inspire and encourage, protect and empower them. As they reach their friends, the adults reach out to their parents through friendship evangelism.

Kids' Slot

Outline

In the intergenerational cell no one is childless. Everyone has the privilege of being the expression of the heart of God to the children of the cell.

A Kids' Slot is when the child(ren) is taken out to another room (or sometimes it may be more appropriate for the adults to go) before the Word and Witness sections of the meeting, until, at an agreed time, they return to the main groups and share together briefly how God moved among them. All cell members take turns to facilitate that time with the child(ren), each member having seen it modelled initially. Those less confident could work with another group member for a season. One of the aims of this time is to build relationships with and among the children, as well as focusing on their relationship with Jesus. Each person needs to be envisioned to share themselves as well as listening to the children. Children love to discover about adults, especially about their childhood! It is not imperative to know all the answers to the questions they may have, 'I'll find out' is a sufficient answer. It is, however, important that each person taking the Kids' Slot comes prepared, having spent time praying for the children and themselves.

Children's co-ordinator

One of the responsibilities of the cell will be to have a children's co-ordinator who will be responsible for

- organising a rota of members to take it (possibly in pairs)
- checking that each home has a place to hold the Kids' Slot (a bedroom, large kitchen, hallway or wherever)
- collecting the materials and ensuring each person has them a week in advance
- organising a book for each person to complete, recording anything that needs following through, problems that need addressing and encouragement, or tips for the next week
- taking a large cloth to each home! This is an invaluable piece of equipment to cover anything in the room that might be a distraction to the children
- reporting back and talking through any problems with the cell leader, keeping the cell leader informed about the progress of the Kids' Slot

Ely example

I would like to share what we, in Ely Christian Fellowship, have done to include our children to the fullest extent. This is a personal testimony, not directive advice! The majority of our children stay in for the whole of the cell meeting, and we find their contributions are invaluable. If a cell is having problems with one or several children the first thing that happens is that a co-ordinator visits.

Most of the time the problem arises because the cell is not being facilitated as it should, and therefore the children are only highlighting the presence of a problem; in which instance there need to be some adjustments for the benefit of everyone. Examples of this are:

- One cell did not give responsibilities to everyone, including the children. Once the children had responsibility and felt valued, their behaviour changed. It was a cell problem, not a children problem!
- Another cell was too large, everyone was having problems!
- One cell was being very uncreative; it was dull for everyone!

However, if the co-ordinator, or children's co-ordinator, has visited and sees that there are age/maturity- or behaviour-related problems that need working through, then a Kids' Slot is introduced for the child(ren) concerned. In our church this is not seen as a permanent situation, but one which is working towards the child(ren) being able to take their place with the rest of the group. This is *never* introduced as a negative experience, or a punishment, and there have never been problems with those taken out, or those left in – everyone is growing at their own pace!

Some groups started with a Kids' Slot for all children and introduced individual children into the meeting with the adults as they were ready.

Options

So, some of the options are
- a Kids' Slot for all children
- start with a Kids' Slot and introduce the children as they, and the group, are ready
- be versatile and have a Kids' Slot for children who would find it difficult in the meeting – many children relate better among adults, while others find it hard

Format

What happens in a Kids' Slot? This may vary from church to church. The following are ideas that you may draw from, but never forget that the aim is for the children to grow as they are empowered to love God, to love one another, to love those who are lost to Jesus.

First, have fun with them, let them get to know you, ask you questions and share about themselves. Share together about the previous week's activities and last week's cell meeting. Then the options are:

- take the same materials as the main cell group, which should already be creative, but change the focus to be totally child orientated. This will maintain the same direction for both parts of the cell group
- or use the *Living with Jesus* series, always ensuring that each

child has their own book and a personal follow up with their 'special friend' (sponsor) during the week
- or have material specially written for your Church. Remember that the children need to address both the Word and Witness sections, just like the adults. Each little one can reach another child, and can be envisioned and encouraged to tell others about Jesus

Remember, even if the children are really small, focus on the fact that each person taking the Slot is building a relationship with each little one and expressing the love of Jesus to them.

Always pray with the children for their areas of expessed need. Remember to let them pray for you, too!

Tips for the intergenerational cell leader

Preparing Always prepare well in advance. Meet with your cell leaders in training prior to the meeting and pray together. The cell leader will need to prepare prayerfully, internalising the programme so it flows and is not stilted. It is good to spend time with the co-ordinator and other cell leaders praying over the coming meetings and sharing creative ideas.

Delegating Always 'model' the meeting for a season before distributing the responsibilities. When you are satisfied that the group has seen you demonstrate the timings and the structure, yet flow in creativity, and when they have seen you prayerfully prepare, then gradually release others to responsibility for specific sections of the meeting. Check that each person prepares well beforehand. They may need help, or coaching, during the early weeks of responsibility. When responsibilities are handed on, the person who had the task for the previous season could oversee the next person for a few weeks. This is good training, teaching each one to raise up another. Encourage people to check that the room in which they will host the meeting is free of toys, and other things that might be the ultimate temptation for children (and young people). A sheet thrown over certain items, such as computers, will be adequate. Arrange seating before people arrive, making sure everyone can see and be seen.

Facilitating The cell leader is a both a facilitator and a participating member of the group. Both of these roles are vital to the success of the meeting. As a facilitator it is important to
- keep the focus off yourself
- develop and encourage interaction between all the members

- notice those who have not contributed and draw them out
- keep a healthy balance of interaction in the meeting

Every leader will take time to develop these skills and to maintain a quiet authority, while not being the focus of everyone's attention.

The other role, that of being an active member of the group, will help the leader as they facilitate. As the leader becomes vulnerable, sharing and allowing others to minister to them, so they

- have their own needs met
- model the way forward to the group
- are seen and known for who they are

So many leaders wear the mask of leadership and suffer under the strain that it imposes on them and their people.

The cell agreement

The cell agreement is literally that! The children and adults enter into agreement about aspects of cell life, so that everyone understands the boundaries and the expectations. These may reflect areas such as discipline, respect, and the cell meeting itself. Just as families have agreed expectations, so the cell will need a uniform agreement for everyone to 'know where they stand'.

Children

The children belong to the whole cell. Show the adults how they can offer positive encouragement to the children to sit with an adult, such as 'Would you help me? I like the ideas you have', or 'I've saved you a space as I want to hear all about . . .' This will enable each child to be helped, should they need it, will make sure they are integrated, and prevent the temptations that arise when they sit in a block together. Should children need encouraging in any particular area, for a limited season small rewards like stickers work wonders, so long as they are given in a meaningful way and every child has the opportunity of obtaining one.

Small groups

During the meeting it is good to break into smaller groups. This may be during the Witness section, for prayer, for ministry, or for parts of the Word section. It is good to do this whenever appropriate for closer interaction, but this strategy will help particularly when

- the group is getting larger
- there are problem people who can monopolise the whole meeting (this localises the problem!)
- the group is not responding as a whole
- the group is looking to the leader to provide all the answers
- there are people who are holding back from participating

INTRODUCTION

It is important that everyone has an opportunity to give or receive. If smaller groups are used during the Word section, it is good to meet up for feedback to the whole group, both to maintain the unity, and for the group to be able to hear how God is moving amongst them all. This, however, need only be a very brief time.

The cell leader should allow himself to be challenged. This is important both during the preparation time and during the meeting itself. If the Holy Spirit has already spoken to the leader before the meeting, the leader will find flowing with Him far easier once the meeting starts.

Feelings   Questions about feelings are important for everyone – adults, young people and children. Everyone has feelings. Feelings are good and acceptable, and are not to be judged. They need to be owned by people. However they do influence our behaviour strongly; how we behave is often determined by what we feel. When applying the Word of God to themselves it is important for everyone to look at the roots of their behaviour. So, being real and honestly identifying feelings is important, and challenging for all ages, bringing repentance, vulnerability, encouragement and revelation.

Bible reading   Decide which version of the Bible you are going to use in the meetings. While children, young people and adults will all bring the version they find easiest, it is important that you have available one that everyone will understand. Read scripture in a lively or meaningful way; the group will see that this brings the words to life, and do the same. Wherever possible, ask two or three different age groups to read from their own versions. This will ensure that everyone hears the Scripture freshly several times, and in a version with which they feel comfortable.

Structure of the meeting outlines

Components   Each series has four components:
- The weekly meeting clearly set out for the cell leader, or cell leader in training.
- Handouts for the cell members where applicable.
- The Kids' Slot material.
- The series delegation sheets. Cell health warning! No part of the meeting should ever be delegated until the group has seen it successfully modelled for several weeks!

Always talk through the materials before the meeting, and

encourage and disciple members afterwards. Generally we have found that it is best to leave the leading of the Word section to the cell leader, or the cell leader in training, as skill and sensitivity are necessary to promote discussion, sharing and for drawing people out.

Remember that the outlines are provided only as a skeleton. They mobilise the intergenerational interaction necessary for a successful meeting, give themes and progression, suggest creative ideas, and make it possible for virtually anyone, whether child, young person or adult, to facilitate most sections of the meeting. It is vital, though, that the materials are used as a tool to promote discussion, and that the bare bones have flesh put on them by a natural flow. Never use them as stilted questions, with stilted answers. Use them for direction, ideas, and 'cues'! When 'for example' is written after a question, this does not indicate that what follows is the right answer because, in many instances, honest answers are the only right answer. The examples are the type of responses for which you are looking. Notes are included to support the Cell Leader, not so he can deliver a Bible study!

It is important to remember that the Cell Leader is a facilitator, and the questions and format are an aid to that facilitating; they are not for simple one-word, or one-sentence answers. However, they are written so that virtually anyone, child or adult, could lead and participate in most sections of the meeting once they have seen them modelled several times. Each person, child or adult, will need varying amounts of support as they learn to take responsibility and develop their giftings.

It is suggested that one meeting series lasts seven weeks, and includes the following:

- a welcome and introduction meeting
- the series outline, which covers four weeks
- a prayer meeting
- a social outreach event

The first week of the series includes a longer Welcome time – perhaps having a bring-and-share meal. This is followed by a shorter 'meeting' time, with an icebreaker, some worship and then the cell leader envisioning the cell about the new series. Each person (and every age group) takes this opportunity to decide what they would like to gain from it, and to look back over the previous series, seeing whether they gained or achieved what they were aiming for.

This is the time to give out responsibilities and distribute the hosting schedule (which should be prepared in advance); to read through and check the cell agreement; to spend time praying together about the series and perhaps praying for members as they assume different responsibilities. The cell can also be told in which weeks the prayer and social outreach are to be held, within the seven week cycle.

INTRODUCTION

Again, small groups of two and three, and creative ideas for presenting these elements, will keep everyone involved and interested.

The prayer meeting

Introduction Children can participate in the prayer life of the cell. Their faith and direct simplicity are essential components of the prayer meeting. When prayer times are creative the children's attention is held, as will be the attention of many more of the adults. Testimonies from adults of different ages and intelligence indicate that, since the children have taken part, the adults enjoy prayer far more than they did before.

Outline Always begin the evening with the Welcome, Icebreaker and Worship as usual! Then move into the time of prayer, using the guidelines below.

Prayer time
- Pray for approximately 10 minutes (no longer than 15 minutes) before changing the topic and manner of praying.
- Pray in twos or threes, which will mean everyone is involved.
- Give everyone 5 minutes to lead on a topic, asking them to bring an activity to go with it. Some children may need help to prepare this, as may some of the adults.
- Pray with action and drama, which can lead into prophetic prayer.
- Give everyone (children and adults) the opportunity to understand fully what is being prayed about by bringing pictures, maps, letters, newspapers, photographs.
- Ask the children to help you prepare, by doing drawings and bringing topics particularly relevant to them.
- Look back and see how God has answered prayer since the last time the group prayed. Children (and adults) love to hear stories of answered prayer – they build faith.
- Include prayer about items that directly touch the children's lives – as with adults, it makes prayer more interesting.
- Put prayer topics in different parts of the house and let people move from one to the other, rather like a treasure hunt, praying for 4 minutes at every place where the prayer treasure is found! (Adults enjoy this, too.)
- Go in twos or threes to different places in the vicinity and pray, such as different public buildings, shops, schools, around the hospital.
- Ask children (and adults) to write letters to local people, such as the fire brigade, police, county councillor, asking what they would like prayer for. Take the letter, wait for a reply then pray over the replies. This could be an on-going project.

- Pray for missionaries and other people you support, encouraging each person write a short letter, or draw a picture, to send to them.
- Do not be age conscious. Some children can cope with more than some adults. Look beyond the incorrect assumptions made about the ability to pray effectively together across the age barrier.

Duration

Encourage the children to participate for as long as the leader feels they are able. This will often not depend so much on the children as on the creativity and variety of the prayer meeting. In some cells this will mean that the children go into another room and perhaps watch a Christian video after a certain length of time. But they always need to be involved for a while.

Weekly cell prayer meetings

There may be times when you want to pray without the children; there may be times you want to pray without some of the adults. Do not be age conscious. Some children can cope with more than some adults. Look beyond the incorrect assumptions made about the ability to pray effectively together across age barrier. Prayer meetings that are regular but shorter are just as effective as long meetings. In Ely, children in our cells are encouraged to attend a weekly half-hour cell prayer meeting.

The social outreach meeting

Introduction　　One week of the seven in each series is designated for social outreach. When the cell first forms, the social week will probably be one where the cell members have fun together and enjoy being with one another. As the members get to know each other better and their numbers grow, this meeting will be the occasion to invite friends to join in and meet the cell in an informal setting. It is a good idea to have a different person responsible for planning this event for each series.

Suggestions　　Ideas for the social event could include
- barbecue
- games evening
- a meal that starts at one house and goes from home to home for the different courses – a 'tramps' supper'!
- a visit to a local place of recreation or interest
- children's activities alongside a time of relaxation for the adults
- dividing into smaller groups and doing something together (make sure these are not groups that spend time together anyway)

Series One: The Lord's Supper

Themes and aims

In Worship, this series focuses on Calvary and Jesus Christ as the perfect sacrifice.

In Word, this series focuses on Calvary and the perfect sacrifice of Jesus. The key Scriptures are:
- Mark 14:32-42
- Mark 14:66-72
- Mark 15:16-20
- 1 Corinthians 11:23-28

In Witness, we focus on friendship evangelism.

Kids' Slot material

The themes and aims of each series are the same as for those who are not in the Kids' Slot, as is the vision statement. Everyone takes part together in the Welcome section and the Worship. Those who leave rejoin the main group at the end of the Witness section to share and pray together before the meeting closes.

Week 1

Preparation

This week you will need
- an attractive container with promises from the Bible written on small sheets of paper (one for each person) put inside it
- handouts copied according to the number of small groups you expect to have
- a tape to play during the ministry (check there is a tape recorder in the home you are going to)
- an attractive container for the offering

Welcome

Icebreaker: If you could change one thing about this past week, what would it be and why would you change it?

Worship

- Read Psalm 136:1-6 responsively asking everyone to say, 'His love lasts for ever.' Sing a couple of praise songs.
- Ask each person to say a very short prayer of thanks, after which everyone should say, 'His love lasts for ever'.
- Sing a couple of worship songs, encouraging everyone to worship with their bodies as well as their voices, by lifting their hands, kneeling, or lying (if there is room). Then pray.

Offering

- Remind everyone that God is a God who gives, and has given far more than we can ever give Him. His promises are always there for His children. While we can take ourselves away from God's promise, God will never take the promise away from us.
- Pray, thanking God for all the promises that He has given us.
- Pass the offering container around, followed by the container holding the promises of God written on small pieces of paper. Let each person put in their offering, and then take out a promise. Each person should read the promise that they have taken out.

Word *(personal application)*

- Tell the group that this series is about Calvary, and the perfect sacrifice that Jesus made for us there. This week we are going to try and take a fresh look at what it meant for some of the people who were there.
- Ask everyone to get into groups of four and give each group one of the two handouts. Appoint one person in each group to facilitate the discussion, i.e. ensure that everyone is drawn into the discussion.
- Ask them to go through part A of the sheet, then ask each group to give a quick feedback to everyone.
- Now ask the small groups to discuss part B, after which return for further feedback.
- Ask everyone how their life will change after taking a fresh look at Calvary tonight.

Ministry

- Play a quiet tape, maybe about Calvary.
- Pray in pairs, asking the Holy Spirit to change us into people who have really been to the cross.

Witness

Vision: Our cell group is where we meet in covenant relationship, with a commitment to 'love God, love each other and love those who are lost to Jesus'. Just as Jesus counted the cost in dying for us, so we need to count the cost as we commit ourselves to Him, each other and those around us.

- Ask each person to think of the friend they are winning for Jesus. What is stopping them from coming to Jesus? Ask the Holy Spirit to show you three things. Do this in pairs if it will be easier.
- Go round the group and ask each person to say the three things.
- Listen carefully and see if groups of similar problems arise; divide people into those groupings and spend a short time praying about these things, and commanding them to go.

Finish   With everyone holding hands in a circle, ask one person to pray about what has happened at this meeting, and its outworking in the lives of the group members.

Handout 1

A

- Your group is to discuss what it might have been like to be Mary, Jesus' mother, at the cross.
- Ask different people to read the following Scriptures: Luke 1:26-36; Luke 2:51-52; John 19:25-30.
- What changing hopes might you have had for your son?
- What might Mary have thought about as she stood at the cross?
- What might Mary have felt as she looked at her son on the cross?
- What might Mary have felt when Jesus asked John to take her to his home?

B

- How do you think you would have felt and behaved if you had been in the same situation as Mary?
- Have you ever been in any situations where you have had to face similar thoughts or feelings?

Handout 2

A

- Your group is to discuss what it might have been like to have been in the crowd on the following occasions. Read Luke 19:33-40; Luke 23:13-23; Luke 23:38-46.
- What different feelings would you have had, and why?
- What different hopes would you have had?
- What do you think you would have thought and felt when the sun stopped shining? (Luke 19:44)

B

- What do you think you would have done if you had been in the crowd?
- Have you ever been in a situation when you have had thoughts or feelings like the people in the crowd?

THE LORD'S SUPPER

Kids' Slot material: Week 1

Preparation

This week you will need
- pencils
- a large sheet of paper
- a marker pen
- a number of small boxes

Begin by chatting together about the previous week, looking back at the previous week's cell meeting and talking through any follow-up, such as concerns they had, or things they were looking forward to. It is always good to relax and share together first, so building relationship with the children.

Word

- Ask a child to read Luke 19:35-38.
- Now suggest the children close their eyes and pretend that they are one of the children in the crowd as you read the passage again.
- What do they think the children would have thought and felt as they cheered Jesus?
- Now invite another child to read Luke 23:32-34.
- Suggest the children close their eyes and pretend that they are one of the children in the crowd watching Jesus being hung on the cross, as you read it again.
- Ask the children what they would like to say to Jesus.
- Write down what each child says on a large sheet of paper. Then read the answers together as a prayer to Jesus.

Witness

- What do the children think stops their friends accepting Jesus?
- Write each answer on a small box.
- Put all the boxes on the floor. Let the children take turns at praying that these obstacles will be overcome by the blood of Jesus, so their friends can come to know Him.
- After each prayer, let them smash the box, so smashing the stronghold written on it! 'Strongholds' are explained simply in *Living with Jesus* Book 5.

Finish

Return to the other group and share the prayer the children wrote on the large sheet of paper. Perhaps the whole cell could pray it together.

Week 2

Preparation This week you will need
- an attractive container for the offering
- handouts for the groups in the Word section

Welcome

Icebreaker: What do you most enjoy doing in your spare time, and why do you enjoy it?

Worship

- Start with a couple of songs of praise.
- Read Psalm 136:1 then verses 6 to 9, with everyone again saying, 'His love lasts for ever'.
- Ask everyone in the group to complete the line 'Give thanks to the Lord who . . .'. After each person's contribution, everyone else should say 'His love lasts for ever'.
- Sing another song of praise or worship

Offering
- Ask someone to read Luke 21:1-4. Discuss why Jesus was pleased with the little that the widow gave.
- Pray, thanking God for the way He gives to us, and asking Him to change our hearts (using the answers that were given by the group).
- Pass the offering container.

Word *(personal application)*

- Remind the group that you are all looking at Calvary for this series. This week you are considering the disciples at Calvary. We are Jesus' disciples and the implications for them are the same as they are for us today.
- Ask people to go into groups of three and discuss part A of the handout, which is about the disciples. Ask each group to tell the others briefly about their discussion.
- Spend a short time talking about what a disciple is, and who are Jesus' disciples today.
- Return to the small groups and look at part B of the handout, then bring everyone back together.
  Having regrets is acceptable, but we need to go a step further

THE LORD'S SUPPER

and think carefully about what we need to change and how we are going to do that, so that we don't have those regrets again. What can we do to help us make those changes? For example, tell Jesus we are sorry and ask the Holy Spirit to help us, or tell another person about the change and ask them to pray for us, and take an interest in how we are getting on (this is called an accountability partner).

Ministry   Ask people to get into pairs (if you have sponsors, special friends or accountability partners present, use those). Then ask everyone to share the changes they need to make, and to pray for each other.

Witness

Vision: Our prayer chain is a vital link that will help us when we need prayer. You can use it by calling the first person on the list and the chain will then be activated. This is completely voluntary and you can have your name and number entered if you wish.

Return to the groups you prayed in last week and share any changes you've seen in the areas you prayed about. Talk about any practical ways you can help each other with these problems.

Finish   Join hands as a cell, and ask some one to pray before you leave.

Handout

A

- This week we are going to discuss what it might have been like to be a disciple with Jesus.
- What might it have been like to have lived with Jesus for three years?
- Ask different people to read Luke 19:33-40; Luke 22:39-51; Luke 23:32-49.
- What changing hopes might you have had?
- What thoughts might you have had?
- What might the disciples have been very sorry, or had regrets about after Jesus had died?

B

- How might you have felt or reacted if you had been a disciple?
- What are you really sorry about, what regrets do you have, as you remember what Jesus did for you at Calvary?

Kids' Slot material: Week 2

Preparation

This week you will need
- a Bible that is easy to understand
- a large sheet of paper
- a marker pen

Begin by chatting together about the previous week, looking back at the previous week's cell meeting and talking through any follow-up, such as concerns they had, or things they were looking forward to. It is always good to relax and share together first, so building relationship with the children.

Word

- Ask a child to read Mark 14:66-72.
- Read the passage again yourself and suggest the children close their eyes and imagine being Peter.
- How do they think Peter felt when he saw Jesus again after He had risen from the dead?
- What do they think Jesus said to Peter when he saw Him?
- Write any appropriate answers on a sheet of paper.
- Ask the children if they ever feel like saying that they do not know Jesus, or if they have ever done that. If they want to repent, allow them to do.
- Encourage the children to read aloud the answers on the sheet of paper, reminding them that what Jesus might have said to Peter He still says to us today when we sin.

Witness

Return to the other group for the witness section and to close the meeting.

WEEK 3

Week 3

Preparation

This week you will need
- an attractive container for the offering

Welcome

Icebreaker: What item of clothing do you enjoy wearing most, and why?

Worship

We have come to worship our King who will be returning!
- Sing a couple of songs about Jesus' return.
- Ask someone to read Acts 1:7-11.
- Go around the group (icebreaker style) and let each person complete the following, 'Jesus, I am so glad that you are coming back for me and I want to tell you that . . .'.
- Sing a couple of worship songs.

Offering

Malachi 3:3 talks about bringing offerings to God 'in the right way'. Ask the group what they think is the 'right way' to bring an offering to God. Ask a child and an adult to pray that we will bring offerings 'in the right way' before taking the offering.

Word *(personal application)*

This week you are going to try and understand a little of what it must have been like for Jesus Himself, at Calvary.
- Ask someone to read Mark 14:32-42.
  What might Jesus have been thinking and feeling? What do you think the Father might have been thinking and feeling? If you have fathers present, ask them how they might have felt if it was their child.
- Ask someone else to read Mark 14:66-72.
  What do you think Jesus thought and felt when Peter said that he did not know Him? Has someone in the group ever desperately needed the support of a friend and not received it? How did it feel?
- Ask another person to read Mark 15:16-20.
  What do you think the cross meant for Jesus?
- Ask everyone to close their eyes for a few moments and in their imagination see Jesus in the centre of the room.

31

Ministry

- Ask someone to read John 3:16.
- Spend a few moments letting everyone say a few words to Jesus.
- Ask everyone to move around from one person to another, and tell them to say something that they know Jesus would say to them (we are His body).

Witness

Vision: Our cell group is a place where we will be committed to building relationship. This will necessitate us being vulnerable and resolving conflicts as they arise. Each group will meet conflict. If this is worked through, each person will reach a place of greater maturity and peace.

- Ask everyone to open their Bibles at John 3:16, then ask them to read it, putting in the name of the person they are reaching out to, for example, 'For God so loved John that He gave . . .'. It does not matter if everyone reads it in a different version.
- Go around every member and let them each just say, 'For God so loved . . .'. Ask one person to pray that each of these people will know the love of Jesus.

Finish

To conclude the meeting ask someone to pray that you will all know the love of Jesus through the coming week.

Kids' Slot material: Week 3

Preparation

This week you will need
- a Bible that is easy to understand
- a piece of paper for each child
- pencils

Begin by chatting together about the previous week, looking back at the previous week's cell meeting and talking through any follow-up, such as concerns they had, or things they were looking forward to. It is always good to relax and share together first, so building relationship with the children.

Word

- Read Luke 22:39-46.
  Suggest the children close their eyes and imagine being Jesus as you read the passage again.
- What do they think Jesus thought and felt at that time?
- Who do the children think that Jesus was going to die for? (See if they personalise it.)
- Ask the children if they know they are that special to Jesus.
- Give each child a piece of paper and help them make a poster that says, 'I am special because . . .' Encourage them to write something that relates to who they are, rather than what they can do!
- Finish by letting each child say, 'Thank you, Jesus. I am special to you because . . .'

Witness

Turn the posters over and write on the back the name of someone they are winning for Jesus. Under the name, complete the statement '. . . is special to Jesus because . . .'

Finish

Return to the other group and share together how both groups have got on.

THE LORD'S SUPPER

Week 4

Preparation This week you will need
- an attractive container for the offering

and, set out in the middle of the room,

- a small table with a special cloth on it
- wine
- bread
- cup
- Bible
- strips of plain paper
- the offering container

Welcome

Icebreaker: Share one thing you know you are good at, and one thing that you find very difficult.

Worship

- Ask everyone to stand and make a circle around the table.
- Sing a quiet song about Jesus.
- Ask everyone to look at the table and pray what comes into their heart. Then suggest that those who would like to, kneel, while a couple of worship songs are sung.

Offering Ask everyone to quietly go forward and put their offering in the container on the table, as the last song is sung again.

Word *(personal application)*

This week you are considering communion before celebrating it together. There are many questions; make sure that everyone is involved. Remember that any honest answer needs to be accepted without judgement.
- Ask someone to read 1 Corinthians 11:23-26.
  Ask what people feel when they take communion, and how important communion is to them. Do they feel happy, sad, bored, unimportant, involved, alone?
- Ask an adult and a child to read 1 Corinthians 11:27.
  What do you think the words 'unworthy manner' mean? For

example, do they suggest not understanding to the best of your ability, or knowing that you have not forgiven someone, or playing around during communion.
- Ask someone else to read 1 Corinthians 11:28.
  How do you examine yourself? For example, do we ask a leader what they see in our lives? Do we ask the Holy Spirit to tell us how we need to change? Do we read the Bible carefully, thinking about our actions and attitudes?

Ministry

Spend a few moments being quiet and letting everyone 'examine' themselves. Offer the opportunity of praying prayers of repentance.
- Ask each person to take a piece of paper from the table, and write their name on it. Focus on the table. Ask everyone to put their paper on the table and then repeat after you, 'We are a covenant people – meeting together, worshipping together and sharing our lives together. We are the body of Jesus for the world to see.'
- Ask a child to read 1 Corinthians 11:23-24.
  Pass around the bread
- Ask an adult or teenager to read 1 Corinthians 11:25-26.
  Pass around the wine.
- Ask everyone to join hands around the table and ask an adult and a child to pray.

Witness

Vision: While we are enjoying forming relationships and developing a healthy cell, we are also committed to growing the cell – to multiply and extend the Kingdom of God. We need to pray for leaders to be raised up among us so that we can be ready to celebrate our multiplication.

Still with hands joined, and standing around the table, go round and ask everyone to pray briefly for their unsaved friends. Then break the circle and imagine the spaces filled with those people. Believe for them to be there, in other words exercise your faith!

Finish

Close the meeting by asking one person to pray.

THE LORD'S SUPPER

Kids' Slot material: Week 4

Preparation

This week you will need
- a Bible that is easy to understand

Begin by chatting together about the previous week, looking back at the previous week's cell meeting and talking through any follow-up, such as concerns they had, or things they were looking forward to. It is always good to relax and share together first, so building relationship with the children.

Word

Ask the children if any of them have completed Book 2 of *Living with Jesus, Special times and gifts*. If they have, those children could share what they have discovered about the Lord's Supper.
- Then ask the other children to share what they know about the Lord's Supper.
- Read 1 Corinthians 11:28, asking the children what they think it means.
- Spend a few moments making sure that the children understand that they need to forgive, and be friends with people, before they take communion. Give them the opportunity to respond to this.

Finish   Return to the other group for the Witness section.

Delegation forms

Series One: The Lord's Supper

Member

_____

Cell Leader

_____

We would like you to do the **Icebreaker** for this series, **The Lord's Supper**.

This will be for _____ _____
(Insert dates)
_____ and _____

Remember that you tell the group what the question is, then answer it yourself before passing it around and giving each person a chance to answer. If anyone has trouble thinking of their answer, come back to them later.

Icebreaker: Week 1

If you could change one thing about this past week, what would it be and why would you change it?

Icebreaker: Week 2

What do you most enjoy doing in your spare time and why do you enjoy doing it?

Icebreaker: Week 3

What item of clothing do you enjoy wearing most, and why?

Icebreaker: Week 4

Share one thing you know you are good at, and one thing that you find difficult.

Member
_____

Cell Leader
_____

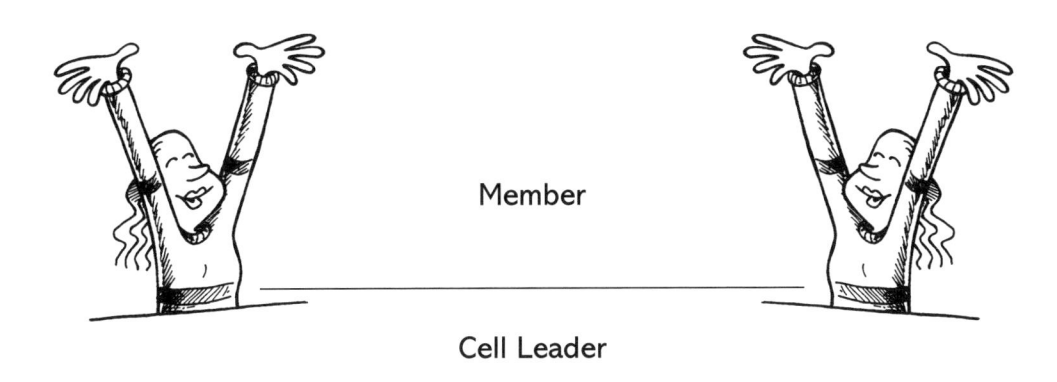

We would like you to lead the **Worship** for this series, **The Lord's Supper**.

This will be for _____   _____
(Insert dates)
_____ and _____

This should last approximately ___ minutes. Songs will need to be easily repeated. If necessary you could have sheets for everyone to use (you could write these and photocopy them). You may like to use tapes that you have pre-recorded, so that songs are in the right sequence. Alternatively you could ask someone to play a guitar (or other instrument), or sing unaccompanied. Be creative – God is a very creative God – just look at the universe!

The following are outlines for the worship time; however you will need to create a flow and invite the Holy Spirit into this framework.

Worship: Week 1

- Read Psalm 136:1-6 responsively, asking everyone to say, 'His love lasts for ever'. Sing a couple of praise songs.

- Ask each person to say a very short prayer of thanks, after which everyone should say, 'His love lasts for ever'.

- Sing a couple of worship songs, encouraging everyone to express their worship with their bodies as well as their voices, by lifting their hands or kneeling.

- Pray.

Worship: Week 2

- Start with a couple of songs of praise.
- Read Psalm 136:1 then verses 6 to 9 with everyone again saying, 'His love last for ever'.
- Ask everyone in the group to complete the line, 'Give thanks to the Lord who . . .' After each person's contribution, everyone else should say, 'His love lasts for ever'.
- Sing another song of praise or worship.
- Pray.

Worship: Week 3

- We have come to worship our King who will be returning! Sing a couple of songs about Jesus' return.
- Ask someone to read Acts 1:7-11.
- Go around the group (icebreaker style) and let each person complete the following, 'Jesus, I am so glad that you are coming back for me and I want to tell you that . . .'
- Sing a couple of worship songs.

Worship: Week 4

- Ask everyone to stand and make a circle around the table.
- Sing a quiet song about Jesus.
- Ask everyone to look at the table and pray what comes into their heart. Then suggest that those who would like to, kneel, while a couple of worship songs are sung.

Member

_____

Cell Leader

_____

We would like you to lead the **Offering** for this series, **The Lord's Supper**.

This will be for _____ _____
(Insert dates)
 _____ and _____

Remember that the offering is part of the worship, so allow it to flow easily from the time of worship.

Take a container for the offering – you could make one, or bring something that is precious to you.

Offering: Week 1

- Remind everyone that God is a God who gives, and has given far more than we can ever give Him. His promises are always there for His children. While we can take ourselves away from God's promise, God will never take the promise away from us.

- Pray, thanking God for all the promises that He has given us.

- Pass the offering container around followed by the container holding the promises of God written on small pieces of paper. Let each person put in their offering, and then take out a promise.

- Each person should read the promise that they have taken out.

Offering: Week 2

- Ask someone to read Luke 21:1-4.
- Discuss why Jesus was pleased with the little that the widow gave.
- Pray, thanking God for the way He gives to us, and asking Him to change our hearts (using the answers that were given by the group) before taking the offering.

Offering: Week 3

- Malachi 3:3 talks about bringing offerings to God 'in the right way'. Ask the group what they think is the 'right way' to bring an offering to God.
- Ask a child and an adult to pray that we will bring offerings 'in the right way' before taking the offering.

Offering: Week 4

- Ask everyone to go forward quietly and put their offering in the container on the table, as the last song is sung again.

Member

_____

Cell Leader

_____

We would like you to lead the **Ministry** for this series, **The Lord's Supper**.

This will be for _____ _____
(Insert dates)
_____ and _____

Remember that the ministry will be part of the Word or the Witness section of the meeting. Keep the flow of the meeting as you move into ministry.

Ministry: Week 1

- Play a quiet tape, maybe about Calvary.
- Pray in pairs, asking the Holy Spirit to change us into people who have really been to the cross.

Ministry: Week 2

- Ask people to get into pairs (if you have sponsors, special friends or accountability partners in place, use those).
- Ask everyone to share the changes they need to make, and pray for each other.

Ministry: Week 3

- Ask someone to read John 3:16. Spend a few moments letting everyone say a few words to Jesus.

- Ask everyone to move around from one person to another, and tell them to say something that they know Jesus would say to them (we are His body).

Ministry: Week 4

- Spend a few moments being quiet and letting everyone 'examine' themselves. Offer the opportunity of praying prayers of repentance.

- Ask each person to take a piece of paper from the table, and write their name on it. Focus on the table.

- Ask everyone to put their paper on the table an then repeat after you, 'We are a covenant people, meeting together, worshipping together and sharing our lives together. We are the body of Jesus for the world to see.'

- Ask a child to read 1 Corinthians 11:23-24.
  Pass around the bread.

- Ask an adult to read 1 Corinthians 11:25-26.
  Pass around the wine.

- Ask everyone to join hands around the table and ask an adult and a child to pray.

Member

_____

Cell Leader

_____

We would like you to lead the **Witness** for this series, **The Lord's Supper**.

This will be for _____   _____
(Insert dates)
_____ and _____

This is about the witness of the group to those who do not know Jesus.

Pray and prepare before you go to the meeting. The devil will be totally opposed to souls being saved, but 'greater is He that is in you than he that is in the world'.

Witness: Week 1

- Ask each person to think of the friend they are winning for Jesus.

- What is stopping them from coming to Jesus? Ask the Holy Spirit to show you three things. Do this in pairs if it will be easier.

- Go round the group and ask each person to say the three things.

- Listen carefully and see if groups of similar problems arise; divide people into those groupings and spend a short time praying about these things, and commanding them to go.

Witness: Week 2

- Return to the groups you prayed in last week and share any changes you see in the areas you prayed about.
- Talk about any practical ways you can help each other with these problems.

Witness: Week 3

- Ask everyone to open their Bibles at John 3:16, then ask them to read it, putting in the name of the person they are reaching out to, for example, 'For God so loved *John* that He gave . . .' It does not matter if everyone reads it in a different version.
- Then go around every member and let them each just say, 'For God so loved . . .'
- Ask one person to pray that each of these people will know the love of Jesus.

Witness: Week 4

- Still with hands joined, and standing around the table, go round and ask everyone to pray briefly for their unsaved friends.
- Then break the circle and imagine the spaces filled with those people. Believe for them to be there; in other words, exercise your faith!

Series Two: Prayer

Themes and aims

In Worship, this series focuses on the names of God.

In Word, we focus on different aspects of prayer.
Key Scriptures are:
- Luke 15:3-7
- Numbers 33:50-53
- 2 Corinthians 10:3,4
- Exodus 17:8-13
- John 17:21-23

In Witness, we focus on prayer walking and friendship evangelism.

Kids' Slot material

The themes and aims of each series are the same as for those who are not in the Kids' Slot, as is the vision statement. Everyone takes part together in the Welcome section and the Worship. Any who leave rejoin the main group at the end of the Witness section to share and pray together before the meeting closes.

Week 1

Preparation

Ask some of the children to come prepared to mime Luke 15:3-7, the parable of the lost sheep. Tell them it is a secret as the rest of the group is going to guess which story it is!

This week you will need
- a large sheet of paper with an attractive border (the banner), which can be displayed each week
- a large marker pen (for the worship)
- an attractive container for the offering
- handouts for the Word section

Welcome

Icebreaker: If you could have a servant to do one task for you each day, what would that task be, and why would you want it done for you?

PRAYER

Worship

Over the next few weeks we are going to think about some of the names of God. This week we will remember that He is called 'Jehovah Jireh' which means 'my provider'.

- Ask some one to write Jehovah Jireh on the banner.
- Sing a song or two about God being our provider or providing for us.
- Ask someone to read Genesis 22:8-10, 13-14.
- In groups of three thank God for being our provider, and thank Him specifically for all that He has provided for you. Go around the group, each one saying , 'Jehovah Jireh, thank you for providing for me'.
- Sing a couple of worship songs.

Offering

Following on from the worship, thank Him for all that He has given, and thank Him for the privilege of giving back to Him out of His generosity to us.

Word *(personal application)*

The theme this week is praying for the lost: looking at the heart of the Shepherd loving and longing for His lost sheep, and then looking at our own hearts, and asking Him to make ours more like His. Ask the children to mime this story and see if everyone else can guess which one it is!

- Ask someone to read Luke 15:3-7.
  How long did the shepherd look for the sheep (verse 4)? Ask each person to name the person they are winning for Jesus, and say how long they have been reaching out to them. How long will we be prepared to go on reaching out to them, or will we get fed up, or lose heart?
- Ask several people to read verses 5-7.
  In groups of three, look at these verses. See what indications there are as to how important it is to Jesus to find those who do not know Him. Ask each group to read their list. How do we feel, and what difference will it make to us, as we hear those lists?
- As we pray for those who don't know Jesus, we need to have the same heart as Jesus. What do you think is in Jesus' heart as He looks for them?

Ministry

Ask each person to name aloud the person they are reaching for Jesus. Then ask the Holy Spirit to touch every person and give them the heart of Jesus for those who are lost.

Witness

Vision: Each of us has a unique circle of friends and relations who may be unbelievers or unchurched. We can introduce them to the network of relationships in our cell, and as we do this, we will show them the love of Jesus in action.

Jesus knew the sheep that was lost, He knew where the sheep was, and what it would need when He found it. We need to know how we can reach people.

- Pass round the handout, telling everyone that this will help them to plan and pray as a group. Ask people to complete the handouts in pairs, helping each other. Ask the Holy Spirit for a promise that you can pray for them every day.
- Collect in the handouts, explaining that you will photocopy them as it will help in planning prayer and outreach events. (You need to keep these as they will help you to pray, and take an interest in individual and group evangelism. They can be an invaluable resource, especially if you keep them updated.)
- Ask everyone to stand, join hands and pray for a few moments for the group members and for those who are named on the papers.

Finish Conclude the meeting by joining hands and asking someone to pray.

Handout

Name of cell member _____

Name of friend who is lost to Jesus _____

Do they really accept you as their friend yet? _____

Are they yet happy for you to talk to them about Jesus? _____

I know that they need _____
_____

I know that they enjoy _____
_____

I have met these members of their family _____
_____

I have met the following people who are their friends _____
_____

This is the promise God has given me for _____ (name)
_____
_____

WEEK 1

Kids' Slot material: Week 1

Important: Stay with the whole cell until the mime has been completed.

Preparation This week you will need
- a Bible that is easy to understand
- a sweet or chocolate to hide
- handouts
- pencils

Before the meeting, hide a chocolate or sweet so it is easily accessible but very hard to find, for instance in your pocket.

Word

- Begin by asking a child to pray for your time together.
- Then ask a child to read Luke 15:3-7.
  Talk together about how long it took the shepherd to find for the sheep.
- Ask each child to name one person they are reaching for Jesus. Then talk together about how long they will love them and pray for them before they give up!
- Ask a child to read Luke 15:8-10. Then you read it, asking a child to mime it as you do.
- Now tell the children that there is a sweet hidden. Let them know the boundaries, for instance no climbing on furniture, going outside, to find it. Then let them start searching for it. Hopefully they will find it really hard and some will stop looking for it! After a while (if no one has found it) call them back together and ask how they felt when they could not find the sweet. Compare how they felt with how Jesus felt, looking for the lost sheep. Give each child a sweet (we don't want them disappointed!).
- Pray together that we will be like Jesus and keep on praying for our friends until they come to Jesus.

Witness

- Help the children to complete the same handout as the other group. If necessary, pair a younger child with an older child.
- Join hands and pray for those named on the paper.

Finish Chat together about the previous week's cell meeting and talk through any follow-up, such as concerns they had, or things they were looking forward to. Then return to the other group and share together.

Week 2

Preparation

This week you will need
- handouts that were completed last week
- banner and marker pen for the worship
- an attractive offering container
- handout about prayer walking

Welcome

Icebreaker: If you could change one thing in our country, what would it be and why would you change it?

Worship

This week we will think about 'Jehovah Shalom' which means 'God our peace'.
- Ask someone to write Jehovah Shalom on the banner, and then ask someone to read Judges 6:22-24.
- Sing a couple of songs either about God being our peace, or giving us peace. Ask everyone to be very still, very quiet and feel the peace of God for a moment. Then suggest they move from person to person, saying, 'The peace of God be always with you'.
- Then ask everyone to say together, 'Jehovah Shalom, thank you for being my peace'.
- Sing a worship song.

Offering

Ask someone to tell the group how giving has made them happy. Pray and take the offering.

Word *(personal application)*

This week's theme is prayer walking and is a preparation for practical prayer walking next week. Satan is very active in taking God's land; we need to be equally active in taking it back.
- Ask someone to read Numbers 33:50-53.
- Ask another person to read verse 53 again.
- What is the land that God has given us to 'take over'? For example, is it the world, our nation, the place where we live?
- As a cell, what is the land that God has given us? For example, is it the streets where we live, our schools, our work places?

- Ask someone to read the verses again and ask some of the cell to mime the passage as it is read. Draw everyone's attention to the violence. We need to be forceful in coming against Satan.
- Ask someone to read 2 Corinthians 10:3-4.
  What are the weapons that we have to use, and how can we use them to the best advantage? For example, prayer, fasting, proclaiming.

Prayer is one of the weapons that God has given us to take back the land. We are going to be prayer walking the streets and taking them back for Jesus. Each street is made up of individual homes. What kind of things can we pray that will help win the land back for Jesus? For example, we can pray:
- for people to turn away from their sin
- for more Christians to move into the area
- for all the children in the street
- for things to happen that will bring people to Jesus
- to demand that Satan stops blinding their eyes to Jesus

Ministry

Ask if anyone needs to be prayed for because they have problems when they walk the streets, such as fear. Pray for anyone who needs it.

Witness

Vision: Prayer is a powerful weapon. It can be used against the powers of darkness on behalf of our unsaved friends and neighbourhood. It is the responsibility of the cell groups, both as individuals and corporately, to be faithful in prayer.

- Tell everyone that next week you are all going to meet at . . . o'clock (your usual Welcome time) and will be walking in groups of three or four down a street near the home where you are scheduled to meet. This is called prayer walking. Pass round the handout. Allow time to read it and ask if there are any questions.

Finish

Ask everyone to join hands while a few people from different age groups pray about the walk the following week.

Handout

PRAYER WALKING

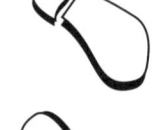

- Takes the Kingdom of God onto the streets
- Helps us to think differently about the way we pray
- Lets us see the places that we pray for
- Shows us things that we would never see praying indoors
- Takes Satan's ground as our feet walk the ground for Jesus

How do we do it?

- By praying outside day or night
- By being on the move, though it is not the distance you cover that matters, it is the prayer
- By talking to God, agreeing with each other, sharing with each other
- By praying about the people, the places, the things that you see
- By praying what the Holy Spirit tells you to pray

Who can prayer walk?

ANYONE!

It is good to do it in small groups, and to pray together before you go out, and when you return.

Kids' Slot material: Week 2

Preparation

This week you will need
- a Bible that is easy to understand
- pictures of your locality such as postcards, newspaper pictures
- paper
- pencils and colouring pencils

Begin by chatting together about the previous week, looking back at the previous week's cell meeting and talking through any follow-up, such as concerns they had, or things they were looking forward to. It is always good to relax and share together first, so building relationship with the children.

Word

- Show the children some pictures of your area. Talk about the pictures, see if the children can recognise them.
- Encourage each child to draw a picture of their street.
- Read Numbers 33:50-53, asking the children to mime it as it is read for a second time. Talk together about what is happening in these verses.
- Read Numbers 33:53 and check that the children understand what is being said; if not, explain it to them.
- Ask what the land is that God has given to us.
- How do the children think that they are going to win back that land for Jesus?
- Share with them about prayer walking.
- Let each child hold the picture of their street and pray for it, naming people they know who live there.

Witness

- Explain that next week you are all going to prayer walk. Ask if any of them have done this before, and let those who have share what happened.
- Explain that
  - we see the things we are praying for as we go outside
  - we become an army, taking back Satan's land.
- Look again at the pictures and postcards of your area which you showed the children earlier. Invite the children to lay hands on each one and pray for that place.

Finish

Return to the other group to pray with them about the following week's prayer walk.

PRAYER

Week 3

Preparation

This week you will need
- a list of streets you are going to prayer walk, in the vicinity of the home which will be hosting the cell meeting
- the banner and marker for the worship
- a tape (or a soloist) for the worship
- an attractive container for the offering
- handouts for the ministry section
- handout from Week 1

Prayer walk

Allow 20 minutes for this. As the group arrive, pray together and send them out in threes to streets you have previously designated. Make sure someone in the group has a watch and state clearly the time to return.

Ask one person to remain behind (maybe the host/hostess) to welcome anyone who might arrive late, and to serve drinks as people return from the walk. Ask them to pray and support the cell as they prayer walk.

Welcome

Allow 15 minutes for coffee and feedback from the prayer walk. Finally, ask everyone to stand. Ask one person to pray, then confess together,

> 'We will take the land, and settle in it,
> because the Lord has given us the land
> to possess.'

Icebreaker: If you could write a book about anything you liked, what would it be about, and what would the title be?

Worship

The name of God for this week is 'Jehovah Rapha', which means 'the Lord is our healer'.
- Ask someone to write Jehovah Rapha on the banner.
- Ask someone to read Exodus 15:26.
- Sing a song about God being our healer, or about healing.
- Ask one or two people from different age groups to give a very brief testimony of healing, then ask them to pray, thanking God for being our healer.
- Play an appropriate song from a tape, or, if you have someone who can sing well, ask them to sing. Pray and invite the Holy

WEEK 3

Spirit to come and heal, and ask the group to expect to feel His healing touch as they sit quietly and listen to the song.
- Either join in the song that you have just listened to, or sing another relevant one.
- Invite everyone to say together, 'Jehovah Rapha, thank you for being my healer'.

Offering

Pray, thanking God that we have the opportunity of giving to Him. Pass the offering round and ask each person to say, 'Thank you, Jesus' as they put their gift in.

Word *(personal application)*

The theme this week is praying for your leaders. Many people understand in their minds that everyone has a very special place, but have not received it in their hearts. As you consider Exodus 17, ask the Holy Spirit to give people an insight into the role God has entrusted to them in the battle for His Kingdom.
- Ask someone to read Exodus 17:8-13.
- Ask another person, who can read quite dramatically, to read it again slowly while adult members of the group mime it.
- What does this passage tell us about leaders when we think about Moses? For example, it tells us
    - he knew clearly what to do
    - he was a good leader because Joshua willingly obeyed him
    - he knew prayer was important
    - he needed help because he got tired
- What does this passage tell us about leaders when we think about Joshua? For example, it tells us
    - he was obedient
    - he depended on others to pray while he was in the battle.
- Who had the most important job, Moses, Joshua, Aaron or Hur? None of them was more important than the other, the battle could only have been won with all of them.
- How important is it that we pray for our leaders?
- Can they do without people who will support them in this way?
- Who will suffer if we do not pray for them?

Ministry

Pass round the handout, then ask people to get in groups of four of mixed age groups, and complete the questions.

Pray for some of the people named from each section. then everyone lay hands on the cell leaders, then the cell leaders in training.

(Note: when the cell leader is being prayed for, the cell leaders in training should 'lead' so accountability is still in place for prophecy and the like.)

Witness

Vision: Ask an adult and a child to say what the cell group means to them. After the testimonies, remind the cell group that as a cell they are expecting to form at least one new cell, and raise leaders for it.

- Ask everyone to look at the handout from two weeks ago, and look at the promise they received for their unsaved friends.
- Go around the group, asking each person to read their promise, and the whole group agree with them for it to be so.

Finish   Close the meeting with everyone joining hands, and ask someone to pray.

Handout

Praying for our leaders

- Who are the leaders who you hardly ever have the chance to speak to?

- Who are the leaders who you meet sometimes, or talk to occasionally?

- Who are the leaders whom you know well and have a lot to do with?

PRAYER

Kids' Slot material: Week 3

Preparation

This week you will need
- a Bible that is easy to understand
- a large sheet of paper
- a large marker pen
- a photo of your cell leaders and your pastor

Begin by chatting together about the previous week, looking back at the previous week's cell meeting and talking through any follow-up, such as concerns they had, or things they were looking forward to. It is always good to relax and share together first, so building relationship with the children.

Word

- Brainstorm with the children about who the leaders are in your Church, for example, cell leader, co-ordinator, pastor. Write the names on a list, or ask the children to draw pictures of them.
- Ask each child, icebreaker style, to tell the group what they know about any one of the leaders. Now ask the children which leaders they do not know very well. Let them share what they do know!
- Read Exodus 17:8-13, then allocate the parts needed to act the story and read it again slowly, allowing the children to mime it as you do.
- Let them share how they thought Moses was being helped to win the battle.
- Explain that your leaders need the children's (and adults') prayers. If possible, display a photograph of your cell leader and pastor. Pray for them in turn, passing the photograph around the circle, so that each child prays as they hold up the photograph.

Witness

Spend some time letting the children talk about what happened on the prayer walk the previous week and how they felt about it. What did they enjoy? What did they not understand? (Feed back these comments to your cell leader later.)

Finish

Return to the other group and share together about your times apart.

Week 4

Preparation

This week you will need to bring
- the banner and marker pen for the worship
- an attractive container for the offering

Welcome

Ice breaker: What was, or is, your favourite subject at school, and why did you enjoy it?

Worship

This week we remember God as 'El Gibbor', the 'mighty God'.
- Ask someone to write El Gibbor on the banner.
- Invite someone who reads with strength and authority to read Isaiah 9:6-7.
- Sing a couple of songs about the greatness of God, and have a clap offering!
- Ask each person to make a declaration of God's greatness by saying, 'Lord, you are great because you . . .'.
- Sing another song about His greatness.
- Organise everyone to shout together, 'You are El Gibbor, the mighty God!'

Offering

Sing the last song again as the offering is given.

Word *(personal application)*

This week the aim is to consider how important was Jesus' prayer for us to be one, and the implications of our unity for the unsaved world.
- Invite several people, from different age groups, to read John 17:21-23.
- What is Jesus praying for the Church?
- Is He praying that we will really be one, so that the world will believe in Him?
- How can we make a difference to those around us?
- People are looking at us; what will they see?
- Ask everyone to get into groups where they can talk about how people see us in those places where we spend most time. For example, groups who are at school, groups who are in employment, groups who are parents.

- What do people see? (*Not* what should people see?)
- If Jesus prayed for us to be loving and caring, showing Him to those who don't know Him, how important is that for us as a cell, and what are we going to do about it?

Ministry Invite someone else to read John 17:21-23.

Return to the groups that you discussed in, and pray about the things you shared, especially the changes that need to be made in your lives.

Witness

Vision: As we plan special events to which to invite our unchurched or unbelieving friends, we need to remember that we can introduce them to our cell at any time. We are inviting them into relationship both with ourselves as Jesus' body on earth, and with Himself.

- In groups of three, share for a short while how the people who you are winning for Jesus are getting on, and how you feel about reaching out to them; perhaps tired, excited, or discouraged.
- Pray about the things that have been shared.

Finish Join hands, and ask someone to pray.

Kids' Slot material: Week 4

Preparation

This week you will need
- a Bible that is easy to understand
- a large sheet of paper
- a large marker pen
- two items, one broken and one complete

Begin by chatting together about the previous week, looking back at the previous week's cell meeting and talking through any follow-up, such as concerns they had, or things they were looking forward to. It is always good to relax and share together first, so building relationship with the children.

Word

- Show the broken item to the children. Ask them whether they would like it. Then show them a similar but unbroken item and ask which they would prefer.
- Ask a child to read John 17:21-23 and find out if any of them know what Jesus is talking about. Share as you need to about Jesus' Church not being divided.
- Draw a large outline of a body. Let the children write their names inside the outline, or draw picture of every person in your cell. Put Jesus as the head.
- Draw a line representing a fracture around one name.
- Ask the children what things might cause that fracture – hatred, unforgiveness, jealousy and so on. Point out that the head (Jesus) will feel the pain.
- How can that hurt to Jesus' body be healed? For example, by forgiving each other, by repenting and changing our minds about what we do and what we think.
- If they are ready, ask them what things they feel that they need to change in themselves so they can help Jesus' body really be one. Then spend a while encouraging them to tell Jesus that they are sorry.
- Finally, talk about ways we can make sure the body never gets broken: by caring for each other, loving each other, being kind to one another in the things we say and do.

Witness

Ask the children how they feel when they talk to others about Jesus. If any of them are struggling, encourage them, look at how they can help each other and let them pray for one another.

Finish

Return to the other group and share together about how both groups got on.

Delegation forms

Series Two: Prayer

Member

_____

Cell Leader

_____

We would like you to do the **Icebreaker** for this series, **Prayer**.

This will be for _____ _____
(Insert dates)
_____ and _____

Remember that you tell the group what the question is, then answer it yourself before passing it around and giving each person a chance to answer. If anyone has trouble thinking of their answer, come back to them later.

Icebreaker: Week 1

If you could have a servant to do one task for you each day, what would that task be, and why would you want it done for you?

Icebreaker: Week 2

If you could change one thing in our country, what would it be and why would you change it?

Icebreaker: Week 3

If you could write a book about anything you liked, what would it be about and what would the title be?

Icebreaker: Week 4

What was, or is, your favourite subject at school, and why did you enjoy it?

Member
_____

Cell Leader

_____

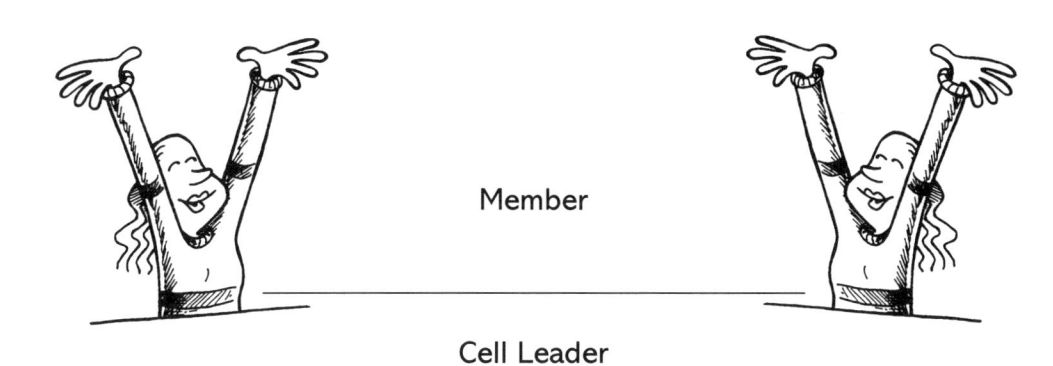

We would like you to lead the **Worship** for this series, **Prayer**.

This will be for _____   _____
(Insert dates)
_____ and _____

This should last approximately ___ minutes. Songs will need to be easily repeated. If necessary you could have sheets for everyone to use (you could write these and photocopy them). You may like to use tapes that you have pre-recorded, so that songs are in the right sequence. Alternatively you could ask someone to play a guitar (or other instrument), or sing unaccompanied. Be creative – God is a very creative God – just look at the universe!

The following are outlines for the worship time; however you will need to create a flow and invite the Holy Spirit into this framework.

Worship: Week 1

- Over the next few weeks we are going to think about some of the names of God.

- This week we will remember that He is called 'Jehovah Jireh' which means 'my provider'.

- Ask someone to write Jehovah Jireh on the banner.

- Sing a song or two about God being our provider, or providing for us.

- Ask someone to read Genesis 22:8-10, 13-14.

- In groups of three, thank God for being our provider, and thank Him specifically for all that He has provided for you. Go around the group, each one saying, 'Jehovah Jireh, thank you for providing for me'.

- Sing a couple of worship songs.

Worship: Week 2

- This week we will think about 'Jehovah Shalom' which means 'peace'.
- Ask someone to write Jehovah Shalom on the banner, and then ask someone to read Judges 6:22-24.
- Sing a couple of songs either about God being our peace, or giving us peace.
- Then ask everyone to be very still, very quiet and feel the peace of God for a moment.
- Ask everyone to move from person to person, and say, 'The peace of God be always with you. Then ask everyone say one together, 'Jehovah Shalom, thank you for being my peace', before singing a worship song.

Worship: Week 3

- The name of God this week is 'Jehovah Rapha', which means 'the Lord is our healer'.
- Ask someone to write Jehovah Rapha on the banner, before asking another person to read Exodus 15:26.
- Sing a song about God being our healer, or about healing.
- Ask one or two people, from different age groups, to give a very brief testimony of healing, then ask them to pray, thanking God for being our healer.
- Play an appropriate song from a tape, or if you have someone who can sing well, ask them to sing. Pray and invite the Holy Spirit to come and heal, and ask the group to expect to feel His healing touch as they sit quietly and listen to the song.
- Either join in the song that you have just listened to, or sing another relevant one.
- Ask everyone to say together, 'Jehovah Rapha, thank you for being my healer'.

Worship: Week 4

- This week we remember God as 'El Gibbor', the 'mighty God'.
- Ask someone to write El Gibbor on the banner, before asking another person, who reads with strength and authority, to read Isaiah 9:6-7.
- Sing a couple of songs about the greatness of God, then have a clap offering.
- Ask each person to make a declaration of His greatness by saying, 'Lord, you are great because you . . .'.
- Sing another song about His greatness.
- Organise everyone to shout together, 'You are El Gibbor, the mighty God!'

Member

_____

Cell Leader

_____

We would like you to lead the **Offering** for this series, **Prayer.**

This will be for _____   _____
(Insert dates)
_____ and _____

Remember that the offering is part of the worship, so allow it to flow easily from the time of worship.

Take a container for the offering – you could make one, or bring something that is precious to you.

Offering: Week 1

Following on from the worship, thank God for all that He has given, and thank Him for the privilege of giving back to Him out of His generosity to us.

Offering: Week 2

Ask for someone to tell the group how giving has made them happy. Pray and take the offering.

Offering: Week 3

Pray, thanking God that we have the opportunity of giving to Him. Pass the offering round and ask each person to say, 'Thank you, Jesus' as they put their gift in.

Offering: Week 4

Sing the last song from your worship as the offering is given.

Member

_____

Cell Leader

_____

We would like you to lead the **Ministry** for this series, **Prayer**.

This will be for _____   _____
(Insert dates)
_____ and _____

Remember that the ministry will be part of the Word or the Witness section of the meeting. Keep the flow of the meeting as you move into ministry.

Ministry: Week 1

- Ask each person to name aloud the person they are reaching for Jesus.
- Then ask the Holy Spirit to touch every person and give them the heart of Jesus for those who are lost.

Ministry: Week 2

- Ask if anyone needs to be prayed for because they have problems when they walk the streets, such as fear.
- Pray for anyone who needs it.

Ministry: Week 3

- Pass round the handout.
- Ask people to be in groups of four, of mixed age groups, and complete the questions.
- Pray for some of the people named from each section.
- Everyone lay hands on the cell leaders, then the cell leaders in training. (Note: when the cell leader is being prayed for, the cell leaders in training should 'lead' so accountability is still in place for prophecy and the like.)

Ministry: Week 4

- Ask someone to read John 17:21-23.
- Return to the groups that you discussed in, and pray about the things you shared, especially the changes that need to be made in your lives.

Member

_____

Cell Leader

_____

We would like you to lead the **Witness** for this series, **Prayer**.

This will be for _____   _____
(Insert dates)
_____ and _____

This is about the witness of the group to those who do not know Jesus.

Pray and prepare before you go to the meeting. The devil will be totally opposed to souls being saved, but 'greater is He that is in you than he that is in the world'.

Witness: Week 1

- Jesus knew the sheep that was lost, He knew where the sheep was, and what it would need when He found it. We need to know how we can reach people.

- Pass round the handouts, telling everyone that this will help them to plan and pray as a group.

- Ask people to complete the handouts in pairs, helping each other. Ask the Holy Spirit for a promise that you can pray for them every day.

- Collect in the handouts, explaining that you will photocopy them as it will help in planning prayer and outreach events. (You need to keep these as they will help you to pray, and take an interest in individual and group evangelism. They can be an invaluable resource, especially if you keep them updated.)

- Ask everyone to stand, join hands, and pray for a few moments for the group members and for those who are named on the papers.

Witness: Week 2

- Tell everyone that next week you are going to meet at . . . o'clock (your usual Welcome time) and will be walking in groups of three or four down a street near the home where you are scheduled to meet.

- This is called prayer walking.

- Pass round the handout. Allow time to read it and ask if there are any questions. Give back the handouts from last week and ask everyone to bring them to the next meeting.

- Ask everyone to join hands and ask a few people from different age groups to pray about the walk the following week.

Witness: Week 3

- Ask everyone to look at the handout from two weeks ago, and look at the promise they received for their unsaved friends.

- Go around the group, asking each person to read their promise, and the whole group agree with them for it to be so.

Witness: Week 4

- In groups of three, share for a short while how the people who you are winning for Jesus are getting on, and how you feel about reaching out to them; perhaps tired, excited, or discouraged.

- Pray about the things that have been shared.

Series Three: Who will be a servant?

Themes and aims

In Worship, this series focuses on Jesus' return and our love response to Him. Who will be a servant?

In Word, we focus on the meaning of servanthood and the example of Jesus.
Key Scriptures are:
- Matthew 12:15-18
- Philippians 2:1-11

In our witness, we focus on witnessing for Jesus.

Kids' Slot material

The themes and aims of each series are the same as for those who are not in the Kids' Slot, as is the vision statement. Everyone takes part together in the Welcome section and the Worship. Rejoin the main group at the end of the Witness section to share and pray together before the meeting closes.

Week 1

Preparation

This week you will need
- an attractive container for the offering

Welcome

Icebreaker: Tell everyone one thing about yourself that might surprise them!

Worship

- Invite someone to read 1 Thessalonians 4:15-18.
- Sing a song about Jesus returning to this earth.
- Ask everyone to say what they think it will be like when He returns. For example, 'When Jesus returns I think it will be . . .' or 'When I think that Jesus will be returning soon I feel . . .'

WEEK 1

- Invite another person to read 1 Thessalonians 4:15-18.
- Sing another song about Jesus' return.
- Ask an adult and a child to pray about His return.

Offering

Talk about the day when we will be able to give Him the crowns that He has given us. For today, we can give Him our love offering. Pray and take the offering.

Word *(personal application)*

Many people say they want to be servants without seriously considering what a servant is. This week is aimed to address that!

- Invite people from different age groups to read Matthew 12:15-18. Then ask another person to read verse 15 again.
- Ask people to go into groups of three and make a list of the ways in which Jesus showed He was God's servant while He was on the earth. Then share the results together.
- Why did Jesus come as a servant?
  - Was it to show us the way, because He loved God and wanted to only do what He wanted?
- What makes a good servant?
  - Is it being obedient, willing, happy?
- Jesus has called us to be servants.
  - How do you feel about being called to be a servant?
- Read Philippians 2:5-8.

Ministry

- In groups of four read Philippians 2:5-8, each reading a verse.
- Ask each person what spoke to them in that reading and why.
- Suggest each person prays about what the Holy Spirit showed them.

Witness

Vision: As we leave our cell meeting, we remember that we are always looking for opportunities to show the love of God through acts of kindness. Whatever age we are, we can always find opportunities to show the love of God to those around us.

- Ask people to describe experiences of sharing Jesus with someone when it went really well, especially how they felt and how the other person reacted.
- Now ask people to share experiences of times when they shared about Jesus and it did not go really well, again particularly how they felt and how the other person reacted.

- Point out to the group that everyone has successes, and failures, everyone feels nervous and so on; but we all need to leave the Holy Spirit to bring people to Jesus, and just be the people who will speak when He asks us to.

Finish   Close by asking everyone to join hands and ask someone to pray before people leave.

Kids' Slot material: Week 1

Preparation This week you will need
- large notebooks for the children
- a Bible that is easy to understand
- pencils

Begin by chatting together about the previous week, looking back at the previous week's cell meeting and talking through any follow-up, such as concerns they had, or things they were looking forward to. It is always good to relax and share together first, so building relationship with the children.

Word

- Ask different children to do a variety of tasks. Ask in a loving way, and say 'thank you' in a very affirming way after each task.
- Let the children share about what they did and how they felt about it. Then ask them if they felt like a servant, and what they think a servant is.
- Invite someone to read Matthew 12:15-19.
- Ask the children if they ever thought of Jesus as a servant.
- Give them each a notebook. On the first page let them draw pictures of Jesus being a servant in different ways, such as healing, feeding people, talking to people, washing feet, dying for us.
- Now ask them what they think makes a good servant (for example, obedience) and write on the second page
     'A good servant . . .'
  and list the qualities they mention.
- Find out if the children realise that we are all called to be servants like Jesus was. Ask them how they feel about that. Let the children pray with each other as necessary.

Witness

- Ask the children to share about a time when they talked to someone about Jesus and it went really well.
- Now ask them to share about a time when it did not go well.
- Help them to see that it is the task of the Holy Spirit to win people to Jesus, and that we all have good times and bad times. We just need to be ready and willing to be the people who speak for Jesus when He tells us to.
- Let them pray for each other as appropriate.
- Finish by returning to the other group and sharing together about the time you have spent.

WHO WILL BE A SERVANT?

Week 2

Preparation

This week you will need
- an attractive container for the offering

Welcome

Icebreaker: Turn to the person next to you and ask them to tell you something about themselves that you don't already know. Then go round the group asking everyone to tell the group what they discovered about the other person.

Worship

- Invite someone to read 1 Thessalonians 4:15-18.
- Sing a song about Jesus' return.
- Ask everyone to turn to the person next to them and share what they think it will be like when they see Jesus on the throne in heaven.
- Ask one or two to share with the whole group.
- Invite someone to read Revelation 4:1-6. Then ask another person to read the same passage while the group close their eyes and 'see' what is being described.
- Quietly start a worship song.
- Suggest someone prays simply and quietly.

Offering

Our offering is part of our worship. Sing the last song again as the offering is taken.

Word *(personal application)*

This week we would like the group to have a greater revelation of the person Jesus really is – not the person we think He is.

- Ask everyone to get into groups of four and read Philippians 2:5-11 verse by verse, sharing after each verse what they've seen about Jesus. Then suggest the groups discuss what they think it must have been like for Jesus to come to this earth as a servant.
- Re-read verses 9-11, then, as a whole cell, talk about why God gave Jesus the highest place in heaven.

Ministry
- Ask three people from different age groups what they think humility is. (N.B.: humility is a strength not a weakness.)
- In groups of three, talk about the things that stop you being humble.
- Spend a short while repenting of those things and asking the Holy Spirit to make us humble like Jesus.

Witness

Vision: As a cell group we are a net. This net is for catching fish. Jesus said He would make us 'fishers of men'. As we move together in community, we are a powerful witness to the love of God.

- Ask each person to say one thing they would like the rest of the group to pray for. It might be connected with their unsaved friend, or it might be their own struggle as they witness for Jesus.
- Pray in pairs for that particular problem.

Finish   Join hands and ask one person to pray before everyone leaves.

Kids' Slot material: Week 2

Preparation

This week you will need
- the notebooks from last week
- a Bible that is easy to understand
- pencils

Begin by chatting together about the previous week, looking back at the previous week's cell meeting and talking through any follow-up, such as concerns they had, or things they were looking forward to. It is always good to relax and share together first, so building relationship with the children.

Word

- Invite a child to read Philippians 2:5-8.
- Ask the children what they thought Jesus was telling us in these verses.
- In the next page of their book, ask them to draw a picture of Jesus in heaven.
- Then ask them to draw Jesus on the cross on the next page.
- Icebreaker style, let each child complete the following, 'When Jesus left heaven I think it must have been . . .'
- Now ask another child to read Philippians 2:9-11.
- Ask them why they think God gave Jesus the highest place in heaven.
- Spend some time letting each child thank Jesus for leaving heaven and dying on the cross for them.

Witness

- Invite each child in turn to share one thing they need help with as they win their friends for Jesus. These may need sharing with other cell members or their parents, as children need support.
- Pray into these areas as a group.

Finish

Return to the other group and share together about how both groups got on.

Week 3

Preparation

This week you will need to bring
- an attractive container for the offering
- taped music for the Worship

Welcome

Icebreaker: Tell everyone two good things about yourself.

Worship

- In pairs, spend a few moments 'writing a letter to Jesus' telling Him how much you love Him.
- Sing a song about loving Jesus.
- Ask half the group to read their letter while quiet music is playing. (You will use the other half next week, so ask them to bring their letters with them.)
- Allow a few moments for people to pray and express their love, then sing another song about loving Jesus.

Offering

Tell the group that this is their 'love offering', and, as you take it, sing one of the previous love songs again.

Word *(personal application)*

This week we are looking at the changes that need to take place in the lives of each member of the group, so that they can be more like Jesus.

- Go around the group and ask everyone to share one sentence about something that they remember from last week.
- Invite one person to read Philippians 2:6-11, then another to read Philippians 2:2-5.
- In groups of three, read verses 2-5 again.
  Suggest each person reads those verses again quietly by themselves and then each share which parts are the hardest for them, and why. Pray for a few moments together then return to the larger group.
- Are we all ready to make the changes we need to make, to be like Jesus?
- What do we have to do for that to happen?

Ministry Stand, grouping the children (if you have them with you) in the middle, with the others around them.

Join hands and pray that the Holy Spirit will fall on each of you, so that you have the power to be like Jesus, as a community together.

Witness

Vision: The place where we work or study is a place of opportunity. As we daily meet and interact with our colleagues and school friends, we are presented with the challenge of living our lives transparently before them. The cell group has the tremendous privilege of supporting its members wherever they work or study.

- Ask each person who is in paid employment to tell the group something about their job. Then ask each of them to say what it is like being a Christian at the place where they work.
- Place a chair in the middle of the floor and invite the rest of the group to place their hands on the people who shared and pray for them.

Finish Close by joining hands and asking one person to pray.

Kids' Slot material: Week 3

Preparation

This week you will need
- the notebooks from last week
- a Bible that is easy to understand
- pencils
- a chair

Begin by chatting together about the previous week, looking back at the previous week's cell meeting and talking through any follow up, such as concerns they had, or things they were looking forward to. It is always good to relax and share together first, so building relationship with the children.

Word

- Look at the second page the children completed in the notebooks this series. Look again at the qualities that make a good servant.
- Ask each child to look at their list and put 'yes' or 'no' against each one depending whether they think they are like that quality or not in their everyday lives.
- Read Philippians 2:5-9 again to show that we are told to be like Jesus.
- Ask the children if they think that God does not notice if we serve others or not. Do they feel that they will loose out if they are God's servants? Encourage them to express honestly how they feel.
- On the next unused page, ask each child to write 'I would like the Holy Spirit to help me to be more . . .' Give them a few moments to pray and ask for help in this area, also confessing their failures.
- Tell them that next week we will share how we got on with those changes in our lives.

Witness

- Place a chair in the middle of the floor and ask one child to sit on it and describe what it is like being a Christian in school.
- Let the other children ask them questions and then pray for them.

Finish

Close by returning to the other group and sharing together.

Week 4

Preparation

This week you will need
- an attractive container for the offering

Welcome

Icebreaker: If you were to die tomorrow, what would you like other people to remember about you?

Worship

- Sing a song about the love of Jesus.
- Ask the rest of the group to read the 'letters to Jesus' they wrote last week.
- Allow a few moments when people can pray and express their love, then sing again about the love of Jesus.

Offering

Do not stop the singing, but quietly pass around the offering.

Word *(personal application)*

Our old way of thinking, in the Church and in the world, is that we serve leaders who are 'anointed' to do the work, but in Cell Church we have a completely different way of seeing, and thinking about things.

Jesus gave us the example of serving others. The cell leaders are servants who humble themselves and serve others. They do not just tell others how they should live, but show them, too, through their own example (see Galatians 2:20).

- Reading around the room, read Philippians 2:1-11.
- Who do we expect to care for us in our cell?
  – Our pastors, the leaders, each other?
- Can everyone care for someone else, or are there some exceptions?
  – How can we care for each other?
- Listen carefully to ideas that come from the group. Implement anything you think may be appropriate, but remember about the sponsor/sponsee relationship, accountability partners, special friends.
- Invite anyone who wants to offer themselves as servants to the rest of the group to stand. Pray for those standing.

Ministry   In groups of three, give people the opportunity of sharing any problems they still have with being a servant. Be ready to help if any group find they can not deal with any problem that arises. Pray in the small groups.

Witness

Vision: Just as we share a love and a concern for the children in our cell, so we need to share the same love and concern for children who have not had the opportunity of hearing about Jesus. The intergenerational cell is a place from which we can reach these children together.

- The aim this week is to find out more about the situations that members of the cell find themselves in, day in and day out.
- Ask the people who shared last week about their employment if they would mind the rest of the group asking them questions about their work and what it means to them to work there.
- Allow people to ask questions – these may vary from being very practical, to very spiritual.
- This time let the rest of the group stand in the middle and allow those in employment to pray for the others as they reach their friends for Jesus.

Finish   Join hands and ask someone to pray before everyone leaves.

WHO WILL BE A SERVANT?

Kids' Slot material: Week 4

Preparation

This week you will need
- the notebooks from last week
- a Bible that is easy to understand
- pencils
- a chair

Begin by chatting together about the previous week, looking back at the previous week's cell meeting and talking through any follow-up, such as concerns they had, or things they were looking forward to. It is always good to relax and share together first, so building relationship with the children.

Word

- Ask the children to look at the last page they completed in their books and let them share together about their progress during the week in the areas that they prayed about, like obedience.
- Invite a child to read Philippians 2:5-9 again.
- Who do they think are the servants in your cell? Who are the people who need to help? Remind them that everyone is a servant in the cell. The cell leader is not expected to do it all!
- Ask them to share ways that the children of the cell can be servants. Then, on the next page of their books, ask them to draw or write ways that the children can be servants in the cell. Remind them to think of the things that Jesus did!
- Encourage the children to pray that they would do these things – serve people – in the same way that Jesus did, willingly, cheerfully.

Witness

- Ask a child to sit on the chair in the middle (a different child from last week) and share about the things they find hard about being a Christian at home.
- Let the other children ask them questions and then pray for them.

Finish

Return to the other group and let the children show the notebooks that they have made, explaining what they are about.

Delegation forms

Series Three: Who will be a servant?

Member

_____

Cell Leader

_____

We would like you to do the **Icebreaker** for this series, **Who will be a servant?**

This will be for _____   _____
(Insert dates)
_____ and _____

Remember that you tell the group what the question is, then answer it yourself before passing it around and giving each person a chance to answer. If anyone has trouble thinking of their answer, come back to them later.

Icebreaker: Week 1

Tell everyone one thing about yourself that might surprise them!

Icebreaker: Week 2

Turn to the person next to you and ask them to tell you something about themselves that you don't already know. Then go round the group asking everyone to tell the group what they discovered about the other person.

Icebreaker: Week 3

Tell everyone two good things about yourself.

Icebreaker: Week 4

If you were to die tomorrow, what would you like other people to remember about you?

Member
_____

Cell Leader
_____

We would like you to lead the **Worship** for this series, **Who will be a servant?**

This will be for _____   _____
(Insert dates)
                _____ and _____

This should last approximately ___ minutes. Songs will need to be easily repeated. If necessary you could have sheets for everyone to use (you could write these and photocopy them). You may like to use tapes that you have pre-recorded, so that songs are in the right sequence. Alternatively you could ask someone to play a guitar (or other instrument), or sing unaccompanied. Be creative – God is a very creative God – just look at the universe!

The following are outlines for the worship time; however you will need to create a flow and invite the Holy Spirit into this framework.

Worship: Week 1

- Invite someone to read 1 Thessalonians 4:15-18.

- Sing a song about Jesus returning to this earth.

- Ask everyone to say what they think it will be like when He returns. For example, 'When Jesus returns I think it will be . . .' or 'When I think that Jesus will be returning soon I feel . . .'.

- Ask another person to read Thessalonians 4:15-18 again.

- Sing another song about Jesus' return.

- Ask an adult and a child to pray abut His return.

Worship: Week 2

- Invite someone to read 1 Thessalonians 4:15-18.
- Sing a song about Jesus' return.
- Ask everyone to turn to the person next to them and share what they think it will be like when they see Jesus on the throne in heaven.
- Ask one to two to share with the whole group.
- Invite someone to read Revelation 4:1-6. Then ask another person to read it while the group close their eyes and 'see' what is being described.
- Quietly start a worship song.
- Suggest someone prays simply and quietly.

Worship: Week 3

Remember to ask everyone to get pen and paper ready during the welcome time– take some spare to the meeting yourself.

- In pairs, spend a few moments 'writing a letter to Jesus' telling Him how much you love Him.
- Sing a song about loving Jesus.
- Ask half the group to read their letter. (You will use the other half next week so ask them to bring their letters with them.)
- Allow a few moments for people to pray and express their love.
- Sing another song about loving Jesus.

Worship: Week 4

- Sing a song abut the love of Jesus.
- Ask the rest of the group to read the 'letters to Jesus' that they wrote last week.
- Allow a few moments when people can pray and express their love.
- Sing again about the love of Jesus.

Member

_____

Cell Leader

_____

We would like you to lead the **Offering** for this series, **Who will be a servant?**

This will be for _____   _____
(Insert dates)
_____ and _____

Remember that the offering is part of the worship, so allow it to flow easily from the time of worship.

Take a container for the offering – you could make one, or bring something that is precious to you.

Offering: Week 1

- Talk about the day when we will be able to give God the crowns that He has given us.
- For today, we can give Him our love offering.
- Pray and take the offering.

Offering: Week 2

- Our offering is part of our worship.
- Sing the last song again as the offering is taken.

Offering: Week 3

- Tell the group that this is their 'love offering', and, as you take it, sing one of the previous love songs again.

Offering: Week 4

- Do not stop the singing, but quietly pass around the offering container during the worship.

Member

_____

Cell Leader

_____

We would like you to lead the **Ministry** for this series, **Who will be a servant?**

This will be for _____ _____
(Insert dates)
_____ and _____

Remember that the ministry will be part of the Word or the Witness section of the meeting. Keep the flow of the meeting as you move into ministry.

Ministry: Week 1

- In groups of four, read Philippians 2:5-8, each reading a verse.
- Ask each person what spoke to them in that reading, and why.
- Suggest each person prays about what the Holy Spirit showed them.

Ministry: Week 2

- Ask three people from different age groups what they think humility is.
- In groups of three, talk about the things that stop you being humble.
- Spend a short while repenting of those things and asking the Holy Spirit to make us humble like Jesus.

Ministry: Week 3

- Stand, grouping the children in the middle, with the others around them.

- Join hands and pray that the Holy Spirit will fall on each of you, so that you have the power to 'be' Jesus, as a community together.

Ministry: Week 4

In groups of three, give people the opportunity of sharing any problems they still have with being a servant. Be ready to help if any group find they cannot deal with any problem that arises, then pray in the small groups.

Member

_____

Cell Leader

_____

We would like you to lead the **Witness** for this series, **Who will be a servant?**

This will be for _____ _____
(Insert dates)
_____ and _____

This is about the witness of the group to those who do not know Jesus.

Pray and prepare before you go to the meeting. The devil will be totally opposed to souls being saved, but 'greater is He that is in you than he that is in the world'.

Witness: Week 1

- Ask people to describe experiences of sharing Jesus with someone when it went really well, especially how they felt, and how the other person reacted.

- Now ask people to share experiences of times when they shared about Jesus and it did not go really well, again particularly how they felt and how the other person reacted.

- Point out to the group that everyone has successes, and failures, everyone feels nervous and so on; but we all need to leave the Holy Spirit to bring people to Jesus, and just to be the people who will speak when He asks us to.

Witness: Week 2

- Ask each person to say one thing they would like the rest of the group to pray for. It might be connected with their unsaved friend, or it might be their own struggle as they witness for Jesus.
- Pray in pairs for that particular problem.

Witness: Week 3

- Ask each person who is in paid employment to tell the group something about their job.
- Then ask each of them to say what it is like being a Christian at the place where they work.
- Place a chair in the middle of the floor and invite the rest of the group to place their hands on the people who shared and pray for them.

Witness: Week 4

- The aim this week is to find out more about the situations that members of the cell find themselves in, day in and day out.
- Ask the people who shared last week about their employment if they would mind the rest of the group asking them questions about their work and what it means to them to work there.
- Allow people to ask questions – these may vary from being very practical to very spiritual.
- This time let the rest of the group stand in the middle and allow those in employment to pray for the others as they reach their friends for Jesus.

Series Four:
Relationships, based on the book of Ruth

Background information for cell leader

You will need to read the book of Ruth, looking carefully at the relationship between Naomi and Ruth, particularly in relation to the sponsor/sponsee relationship in the Cell Church. Make notes of the revelations you get so that you can use them in the cell meeting. The following are just some verses to get you going!

Key verses

Original

Ruth 1:6
Naomi was returning to the land where God visited His people and where his provision could be seen

Ruth 1:16
Ruth chose to be committed to God and Naomi

Ruth 1:20-22
Naomi had troubles of her own, but could still commit to Ruth

Ruth 1:22
Ruth was going to a country whose people, language, customs, law etc. she did not understand.

Ruth 1:22
Ruth did not know if she was going to be accepted by the inhabitants.

Ruth 2:2
Ruth was accountable to Naomi who had more experience of the country and people

Ruth 2:8
Naomi had Ruth's best interests at heart

Cell parallel

Kingdom of God

God and the sponsor

We do not have to be trouble-free before we can sponsor anybody

When becoming a member of the cell/ Kingdom of God a new believer may not understand the language and customs

New people coming in do not know if they are going to be accepted in the cell

The sponsee has the experience of the sponsor to draw on

The sponsor has the sponsee's best interests at heart

Ruth 2:9
Ruth's safety was ensured because she submitted to God and Naomi

The sponsee will equally be safe in submitting to God and to sponsor

Ruth 2:11
The relationship was give and take on both sides

So it is with the sponsor and sponsee

Ruth 2:12
Ruth drew on and trusted in Naomi's wisdom and experience

So it should be with the sponsor and sponsee

Ruth 2:9
Naomi trusted Ruth to go out into the land on her own but, because of the trust relationship, felt able to ask her what had happened on her return

The sponsee will 'go out' alone, but their safety and strength lies in the openness and honesty of the sponsoring relationship

Ruth 3:1-3
Naomi's experience enabled her to give wise counsel to Ruth. Remember they had returned to the place where they were under the rule and provision of God (see 1:6)

Giving wise counsel involves staying submitted, prayerful and in the place where the sponsee hears God as well as drawing on the counsel of the sponsor

Ruth 3:5
Naomi had won Ruth's respect. She responds by behaving with simple obedience

Sponsor should win sponsee's respect and therefore their obedience

Ruth 4:13
Naomi and Ruth both benefited from their relationship

The sponsor/sponsee relationship should be mutually beneficial. It does not have to be one-sided

Matthew 1:5; 1:16
What fruit came from that relationship!

You just never know what God is planning!

Beforehand In the three weeks prior to starting the series on Ruth, ask the group to read through the book of Ruth either with their children, as a family, with another member of the group, or by themselves. You will need to check that this is happening! Another alternative is for the children's ministry to prepare them for this.

Tell them that in the cell meeting you will all be looking at the friendship/relationship between Naomi and Ruth.

Themes and aims

In Worship, this series focuses on thanksgiving.

In Word, we focus on the friendship (relationship) between Naomi and Ruth and apply it to our own friendships. NB 'Friendship' is a good word to use instead of 'relationship', as everyone understands it and can relate to it. Finally, in week 4, we relate Naomi and Ruth's friendship to sponsoring.

In Witness, we focus on friendship evangelism.

Kids' Slot material — The themes and aims of each series are the same as for those who are not in the Kid's Slot, as is the vision statement. Everyone takes part together in the Welcome section and the Worship. Rejoin the main group at the end of the Witness section to share and pray together before the meeting closes.

Week 1

Preparation — Ask the best storyteller in the cell to come prepared to give a lively, creative overview of the story in this first week, lasting no more than 10 minutes. He/she may want to involve other members of the cell.

This week you will need
- an attractive offering container
- a small piece of paper for each member
- an attractive basket/container for the Witness section of the meeting

Welcome

Icebreaker: What did you do that gave you the most fun in the last few weeks?

Worship

- Read Psalm 148:1-12, letting each person read a verse, then repeat verse 12 several times.
- Sing a praise song together, repeating the song as appropriate.

WEEK 1

- Invite each person to say a brief prayer, thanking Jesus for something He has done for them this week. Conclude with the statement, 'Young men and maidens, old men and children, let them praise the name of the Lord!'

Offering

Before taking the offering, ask someone to give a testimony of how God has given to them because they have given faithfully to Him.

Word *(personal application)*

This first week is a general overview, allowing people to identify relationships similar to that of Ruth and Naomi. Tell the group that they are going to be looking at Naomi and Ruth's friendship for this series. Then ask the person you previously arranged with to give the creative overview of the story (10 minutes maximum).
- What did you find out when you looked at the true story of the friendship of Ruth and Naomi? It is fine to keep the discussion very general at this point, as you will be going into it more deeply in the following weeks.
- Can anyone tell us about someone in their life who has been like Naomi to them? For instance, someone who has taught you a lot as you have spent time with them, someone you look up to, or someone you would do anything for because of what they have done for you? Children may say 'their parents', so may adults, and that is an acceptable answer.
- Can anyone tell us about someone who has been like Ruth to you? For instance, someone you have spent a lot of time helping when they needed you, someone who looks up to you, someone who you helped and then became your friend?
- Ask someone to read Matthew 4:18-22.
- What was Jesus looking for in His friends? People who would stand by Him, help Him, listen to Him, share with Him? (You could brainstorm this and write the answers on a large sheet of paper.) Are we looking for the same things in our friendships?

Ministry

This may have opened up wounds in people who feel that they do not have friends, or who have been hurt by friends.
- Ask the group to get into groups of three and pray for each other about friendship. Each person can share what they would like prayer for in the area of friendships.

Witness

Vision: The cell group is a place where we can support each other. Each of us has the ability to encourage another. We will each have someone to whom we can relate closely; this will be called a sponsor/sponsee relationship, and together we will use materials that will help us to grow in our walk with God.

- Stay in the small groups and share how you are getting on in friendships with people you are reaching out to. Each person write their friend's name on a piece of paper.
- Bring the group back together and put all the names in the basket. Invite one adult and one child to pray over all the names in the basket.
- Remind everyone that our commission is to 'love God, love each other and love those who are lost to Jesus'.

Finish Close by asking everyone to stand and hold hands, while one member prays for the group.

Kids' Slot material: Week 1

As a model is going to be made over the next four weeks, it is important to talk to the other three people who will be taking the Kid's Slot over that period and plan the materials and stages of the model making.

Preparation

This week you will need
- a Bible that is easy to understand
- paper
- pencils
- basket (or similar)
- lively music

Begin by chatting together about the previous week, looking back at the previous week's cell meeting and talking through any follow-up, such as concerns they had, or things they were looking forward to. It is always good to relax and share together first, so building relationship with the children.

Word

- Pray together and share any news from the previous week – share your news too!
- Check that the children are aware of the story of Ruth and Naomi. Review it in a creative way: for instance, take it in turns to tell the story letting each child tell a part; take a picture book version and encourage the children say what is happening in the pictures; let them mime the story as you tell it.
- Start making a model of the story of Ruth and Naomi. This will be added to over the four weeks, to be completed on week 4.
- Read Ruth 1:3-19, perhaps while they are working on the model.
- Share with the children about someone in your life who has been like a Naomi, or a Ruth to you. They will enjoy hearing your story!
- Ask the children to share about someone who has helped them to know Jesus better, their 'Naomi', maybe a cell leader, a parent, a special friend (sponsor).
- Invite the children to pray for the people who have helped them, mentioning them by name.
- If any child feels they have no one special like that, affirm them there and then. Afterwards, ask an adult who cares about this child to show them that they really care before the child goes home, and to continue to show that care in the coming weeks.

Witness

- Invite the children to share how they are getting on with the friends they are winning for Jesus.
- Ask each child to write their friend's name, or draw their picture, on a piece of paper.
- Put the papers in a basket and pass it round while playing some music. When the music stops, the person with the basket takes out a name and prays for that person. When you have finished, keep the names for next week.
- Ask the children to repeat after you, 'We will love God, love each other and love those who are lost to Jesus'. This could end with a big cheer!

Finish   Return to the other group and share what Jesus has done for both groups.

Week 2

Preparation

This week you will need
- an attractive offering container
- a praise song that has been recorded several times on the same tape
- large sheet of paper with Moab written in top left hand corner, and Bethlehem written in bottom right hand corner
- two different coloured marker pens
- the basket from the previous week with the names of unsaved people in

Welcome

Icebreaker: Name one thing that you would like to receive from the cell, and one thing that you can give to the cell.

Worship

- Start by exhorting the group as you say Psalm 148:12.
- Play a praise song on tape, and ask everyone to begin to praise God as they listen to the song. Encourage the group to stand and join in as the song is repeated several more times on the tape.
- Invite each member to share what they felt as they praised God – for example, happy, sad, thankful. This could be done icebreaker style, with you sharing first and then going round the group.
- Give people an opportunity to pray before singing another praise song.

Offering

Ask the group to spend a few moments speaking out some of the things God has been given them, for example, homes, work, friends, parents, toys, health. Then take the offering and pray a simple prayer thanking God for His goodness to us and thanking Him for accepting our offering as a token of our thanks.

Word *(personal application)*

This week we are looking at what it felt like for Ruth and Naomi to leave the land of Moab.
- Review the story of Ruth and Naomi creatively.

For example
- by going round the group letting everyone tell a part of the story
- ask a family to act it
- invite the children to show the group a picture that they have drawn of the story

- What might Ruth have felt leaving Moab and going to Bethlehem, and why?
  - Scared and unsure because she did not know what the future held, and did not know the people or the customs of the land? (Ruth 1:22)
  - Sad because she was leaving her own land that had been home to her?
  - Hopeful as she was going a land where God was providing for His people? (Ruth 1:6)
- What might Naomi have felt taking Ruth back with her?
  - Responsible for the care of Ruth? (Ruth 1:16)
  - Nervous – would the people of Bethlehem accept her?
  - Grateful to Ruth for going with her?
- Display the large sheet of paper with Moab and Bethlehem on, and add the responses of the group, one colour for Ruth and another for Naomi. (Here italics for Ruth and roman for Naomi.)
  For example:

MOAB

Sad – she was leaving her old life
Trusting of Naomi.
Scared. Unsure.

Glad Ruth was coming.
Responsible – will I be able to help Ruth?

Nervous – will I be accepted?
Excited.

Nervous – will they accept Ruth?
– will Ruth accept my help?
I've got troubles of my own.

BETHLEHEM

- What would it mean to you to have a friendship like this? Encourage the group to share what they really feel. Are they scared, happy, not wanting the responsibility, too busy, have already got one?

Ministry

In pairs, read Romans 12:9-13 and then ask the Holy Spirit to speak to you. Share how you need to change to become a better friend.
- Pray together about this.
- We are to love God, love each other and love those who are lost to Jesus.

Witness

Vision: As new members come into the cell group, we will be able to encourage them. As we enter into sponsoring relationships with them, we will be able to take them on a journey that we ourselves have been on with another person.

- Pass round the basket with the names in and ask everyone to take out a name.
- Go round the group each praying just one sentence about the person whose name they drew out. It does not matter if the person praying does not know the name, or anything about the person named.
- Each find the person who originally wrote the name on the paper and add one need of that person to the paper, for example a need for friends, for healing, for money.
- Agree in prayer for that need to be met, and see if there is anything that the group could do to meet that need in an appropriate way.
- Share as a whole group if there are needs that the whole group needs to address.
- Collect in the pieces of paper.

Finish   Close with everyone joining hands and ask someone to pray.

Kids' Slot material: Week 2

Preparation

This week you will need
- a Bible that is easy to understand
- the materials needed to complete stage 2 of the model
- a large sheet of paper
- a marker pen
- names and basket from the previous week
- pencils
- lively music

Remain with everyone else until the story of Ruth and Naomi has been reviewed.

Begin by chatting together about the previous week, looking back at the previous week's cell meeting and talking through any follow-up, such as concerns they had, or things they were looking forward to. It is always good to relax and share together first, so building relationship with the children.

Word

- Pray together and share any news from the previous week – share your news too!
- Continue with the second stage of the model. Read Ruth 2:1-9, perhaps while the children are working on the model.
- Display a large sheet of paper. Ask one child to draw a picture of Moab in the top square, and another child one of Bethlehem in the bottom square. Another child could draw a picture of Ruth and Naomi leaving Moab, but ask them not to draw their facial expressions.

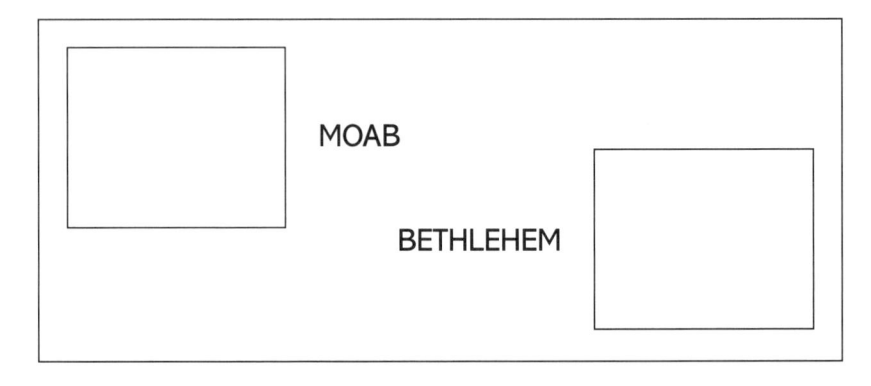

MOAB

BETHLEHEM

- Talk about how Ruth might have felt leaving Moab and how Naomi might have felt leaving Moab. Then draw in their facial expressions, when the children have agreed about what they might have felt.
- Let each child name a close friend and pray for them.

Witness

- Invite the children to repeat after you, 'We will love God, love each other and love those who are lost to Jesus'. This could end with a big cheer!
- Pass the basket from last week round as music is played, and let the person who is holding it when the music stops take out a name. They can ask the person who knows the one named on the paper to tell them something about that person. This information should be written on the back of the paper. Continue to do this until all the papers have been taken out.
- Let each child pray for the person on the paper they are holding, even though they may not know them personally, and mention the information on the back of the paper.

Finish   Return to the rest of the cell and share together.

Week 3

Preparation

This week you will need
- the large sheet of paper from last week
- pieces of paper used in the Witness section from last week
- an attractive container for the offering

Welcome

Icebreaker: What are two of your most precious possessions, and why are they precious to you?

Worship

- Ask someone to read Psalm 150.
- Sing a couple of songs of praise. Encourage everyone to stand up and express their joy in their God.
- Spend a few moments inviting one or two to share something of what God means to them.
- Ask a couple of people of different ages to pray, thanking God for all that He is to us.
- Conclude this time with a short worship song.

Offering

Spend a few moments asking everyone to share ways in which they have seen God provide financially for the Church. Invite each person to pray and thank God after they have shared. Then take the offering.

Word *(personal application)*

This week you are looking at Naomi and Ruth's friendship and asking whether your cell as a whole offers those qualities to individuals. We are corporately the body of Christ, and, as that community, we express Jesus to each other.

- Ask a child to explain to everyone what is on the large sheet of paper. (This will be a good check that everyone understands.)
- This week you are looking at the relationship that existed between Naomi and Ruth.
- What was the friendship between Naomi and Ruth like? Write ideas on the sheet.

```
┌─────────────────────────────────────────────────┐
│  ┌─────────┐   Sad – she was leaving her old life
│  │  MOAB   │   Trusting – of Naomi.
│  └─────────┘   Scared. Unsure.
│  Glad Ruth was coming.
│  Responsible – will I be able to help Ruth?
│
│       They were accountable to each other (Ruth 2:2).
│         Ruth was obedient to Naomi (Ruth 3:5).
│         They had an open friendship (Ruth 2:19).
│      They both benefited from the friendship (Ruth 4:13, 16).
│              They stuck by each other.
│               They loved each other.
│              They trusted each other
│
│                       Nervous – will I be accepted?
│                                            Excited.
│  I've got troubles of my own.          ┌──────────┐
│  Nervous – will they accept Ruth?      │BETHLEHEM │
│       – will Ruth accept my help?      └──────────┘
└─────────────────────────────────────────────────┘
```

- Now ask everyone to think about friendships in the cell and compare them with what is on the large sheet of paper.
  How many of these qualities are present in the group?

- Since we are a body, no one person has to meet every requirement, but the group as a whole has a lot to offer. The following questions might help the group to keep it on a personal level:
  – Who can you tell when you are in trouble?
  – Do you know when someone needs help, or wants to share their happiness?
  – Who would you allow to correct you and point out your mistakes?
  – Who can you share your feelings with?
  – Who do you trust at all times?
  – Of whom can you say that your friendship will last through conflict?
- Read Romans 12:9-16, each person reading a verse.

Ministry Love God, love each other, love those who are lost to Jesus.
Spend time letting the group move around and pray for different people – just a few minutes with each person. Pray that love flows between you all.

Witness

Vision: Children, too, need that special relationship with another person who will walk beside them, *Hand in Hand!* This will usually be a parent, though it may be another 'special friend'. They too have materials that will provide them with a track to move along on their journey with Jesus.*

- Lay all the pieces of paper with the names on the floor or a table in the centre.
- Invite each person to spend 30 seconds giving the rest of the group an update on their friend's situation.
- Ask everyone to pick up one piece of paper and pray for the person named on it for one minute. Repeat this, asking everyone to exchange papers. This can be repeated several times. It is fun and effective!

Finish Close with everyone joining hands and ask someone to pray.

*For details of other cell material, see Appendix 2.

Kids' Slot material: Week 3

Preparation

This week you will need
- a Bible that is easy to understand
- materials for stage 3 of the model
- the pieces of paper with names on from last week
- a piece of card for each child
- pencils

Begin by chatting together about the previous week, looking back at the previous week's cell meeting and talking through any follow-up, such as concerns they had, or things they were looking forward to. It is always good to relax and share together first, so building relationship with the children.

Word

Pray together and share any news from the previous week – share your news too!

- Continue with stage 3 of the model.
  Read Ruth 2:14-23, perhaps while the children are working on the model.
- Now invite a child to draw Ruth and Naomi getting near to Bethlehem, but ask them not to draw their faces.
- Ask the children, what might Ruth have felt as they got to Bethlehem? What might Naomi have felt as they got to Bethlehem?
- Draw in their facial expressions when the children have agreed about what they might have felt.
- Encourage the children to talk about their friends in the cell. Encourage them think generationally, not just about their peers.
- Let them make a small card thanking another person in the cell for their friendship. When the card is finished, invite the child to hold the card and pray for that person.

Witness

Ask the children to repeat after you, 'We will love God, love each other and love those who are lost to Jesus'. Let them tell you what the most difficult bit of that statement is for them. Talk about it and pray for each other.

Finish

Return to the rest of the cell and give the thank you cards to the relevant people and tell them you prayed for them.

Week 4

Preparation

This week you will need
- small items, one for each person, to use inspirationally for the praise and worship. Examples might include a leaf, a key, a coin, a sweet
- the large sheet of paper from last week
- an attractive container for the offering

Welcome

Icebreaker: If someone was coming to our cell meeting for the first time, and you wanted to give them a gift which symbolised what our group was like, what would it be, and why?

Worship

- Give each person one of the items you bought with you.
- Ask them what the object they are holding reminds them to thank God for. Give people a few moments to think about it.
- Go round the group, inviting each one to complete the sentence, 'Thank you, Jesus . . .' For example, a sticking plaster might prompt one to pray 'Thank you, Jesus, for your healing'.
- Sing a song that gives thanks to God. Sing it as many times as the Holy Spirit leads you to.
- Read a Scripture about giving thanks to God, then sing another couple of praise songs.

Offering

Ask someone to read Malachi 3:8-12, then ask, 'What do you think God is saying to us right now through these verses?'

Pray and pass around the offering container.

Word *(personal application)*

This week you are looking at the sponsoring relationship, vital for both the new believer and the accountability partners. By looking at the values that underlie these relationships, the cell will have a greater understanding of their importance.

- Place the large sheet of paper with the groups' thoughts on Ruth and Naomi in the centre of the room. In groups of three or four, share how the past few weeks have changed your friendships.
- Cross out 'Moab' and put 'Kingdom of the World'.
- Cross out 'Bethlehem' and put 'Kingdom of God'.
- What does the visual aid mean to us now?

We are now looking at Moab as being the kingdom of the world and all the feelings that Ruth had could be those of a new Christian coming to the cell, starting a new life in the Kingdom of God. Similarly, the feelings that Naomi had could be those of a cell member when they bring a new believer into the Kingdom of God, and introduce them to the cell.

- Does anyone remember feeling like Ruth when they became a Christian – not understanding what was happening, the 'language and customs'?
- What are the things that new Christians might find hard to understand?
- What can we do to help these people as they become part of our cell?
- How do you feel about people coming into our cell who behave differently from us – uncomfortable, embarrassed, glad to see them, sad?
- In groups of three or four, read 1 Corinthians 13:1-7.
  How can these verses change our attitude to others joining our group?
- Return as a whole group and ask
  – would you help another as Naomi did?
  – would you like to be helped as Ruth was?
- Talk to the group about sponsoring, pointing out that the relationship between Ruth and Naomi was similar to a sponsoring relationship.
- Pass round the handout and talk it through. Have copies of the equipping tracks for adults, young people and children available. Allow time for questions.
- Do not organise accountability partners, or sponsors/cell mates/special friends in the meeting. Take time to pray and talk to people about this. Parents will need consulting. However, it is important to respond to this within the next week.

Witness

Vision: We should always remember that we are being equipped so that we can equip others; we are being nurtured so that we can nurture others; we are bring prayed for so that we can pray for others. The cell group is a place for receiving and giving.

- Spend some time letting people look at the sponsoring materials. Talk them through these and answer questions.
- Love God, love each other, love those who are lost to Jesus.

Finish   End the meeting by asking everyone to stand and join hands, then ask someone to pray.

SPONSORING/BEFRIENDING/DISCIPLING

This is the commitment of building relationships and working through a series of books together: *The Equipping Track* for adults, *Passion for Youth,* and *Living with Jesus* series for children.

It is sharing your life, the ordinary events like mending the car, going shopping, taking the children out. 'Modelling' is showing how a Christian reacts in life's everyday circumstances when under stress, in relationships and so on.

It is allowing the other person to share their life with you, and you taking an interest in things and people that are important to them.

It may be some special outings, but these are not the 'grass roots' learning experiences.

It is being open and accountable to the Cell Leader, or another appointed person.

After sponsoring has finished there is then an

Accountability partner

This is someone in the group who you commit to meeting with weekly, developing an open and trusting relationship with unconditional love for each other.

It means you and your partner working towards being able to speak into each other's lives and be open with one another.

It means asking how you can help each other, and praying for each other.

Kids' Slot material: Week 4

Preparation This week you will need
- a Bible that everyone can understand
- the materials you will need to complete the model of Ruth and Naomi
- display sheet from previous weeks
- a marker pen

Begin by chatting together about the previous week, looking back at the previous week's cell meeting and talking through any follow-up, such as concerns they had, or things they were looking forward to. It is always good to relax and share together first, so building relationship with the children.

Word

- Pray together and share any news from the previous week – share your news too!
- Finish the model of Ruth and Naomi.
- Show the display sheet of Moab and Bethlehem. Paste a piece of paper over Bethlehem and draw each member of the cell on that piece of paper. Draw a picture of a child, without any facial expression, walking toward that piece of paper.
- Talk about what it might feel like to be a child coming into the cell for the first time, and how we can help them to feel at home in this strange 'country'. Then put the relevant facial expression on the child.

Witness

Talk to the children about having someone (possibly their parent) as a special friend (sponsor) to them, just like Naomi was to Ruth. Help them to understand that we all need to help each other. They will be a help to their special friend too.

If possible, have the *Living with Jesus* series available to show them. Let them have a look at the books and be enthusiastic as you explore them together. If the child expresses a desire to do this series, tell your cell leader.

Finish Show the rest of the cell the model and the display sheet. Ask to see their display sheet too!

Delegation forms

Series Four: Relationships, based on the book of Ruth

Member

_____

Cell Leader

_____

We would like you to do the **Icebreaker** for this series, **Relationships, based on the book of Ruth.**

This will be for _____ _____
(Insert dates)
_____ and _____

Remember that you tell the group what the question is, then answer it yourself before passing it around and giving each person a chance to answer. If anyone has trouble thinking of their answer, come back to them later.

Icebreaker: Week 1

What gave you the most fun in the last few weeks?

Icebreaker: Week 2

Name on thing you would like to receive from the cell, and one thing you can give to the cell.

Icebreaker: Week 3

What are two of your most precious possessions, and why are they precious to you?

Icebreaker: Week 4

If someone was coming to our cell meeting for the first time, and you wanted to give them a gift that told them what our group was like, what would it be, and why?

Member
_____

Cell Leader
_____

We would like you to lead the **Worship** for this series, **Relationships, based on the book of Ruth.**

This will be for _____   _____
(Insert dates)
_____ and _____

This should last approximately ___ minutes. Songs will need to be easily repeated. If necessary you could have sheets for everyone to use (you could write these and photocopy them). You may like to use tapes that you have pre-recorded, so that songs are in the right sequence. Alternatively you could ask someone to play a guitar (or other instrument), or sing unaccompanied. Be creative – God is a very creative God – just look at the universe!

The following are outlines for the worship time; however you will need to create a flow and invite the Holy Spirit into this framework.

Worship: Week 1

- Read Psalm 148:1-12, letting each person read a verse, then repeat verse 12 several times.

- Sing a praise song together, repeating the song as appropriate.

- Ask each person to say a brief prayer, thanking Jesus for something He has done for them this week.

- Conclude with the statement, 'Young men and maidens, old men and children, let them praise the name of the Lord!'

Worship: Week 2

- Start by exhorting the group as you say Psalm 148:12.
- Play a praise song on tape, and ask everyone to begin to praise God as they listen to the song.
- Encourage the group to stand and join in as the song is repeated several more times on the tape.
- Invite each member to share what they felt as they praised God – for example, happy, sad, thankful. This could be done icebreaker style, with you sharing first and then going round the group.
- Give people an opportunity to pray before singing another praise song.

Worship: Week 3

- Ask someone to read Psalm 150.
- Sing a couple of songs of praise. Encourage everyone to stand up and express their joy in their God.
- Spend a few moments asking one or two to share something of what God means to them.
- Ask a couple of people of different ages to pray, thanking God for all that He is to us.
- Conclude this time with a short worship song.

Worship: Week 4

- Give each person one of the items you brought with you.
- When you look at the object you are holding, what does it remind you to thank God for? Give people a few moments to think about it.
- Go round the group, inviting each one to complete the sentence, 'Thank you, Jesus . . .' For example, a sticking plaster might prompt one to pray 'Thank you, Jesus, for your healing'.
- Sing a song that gives thanks to God. Sing it as many times as the Holy Spirit leads you to.
- Read a Scripture about giving thanks to God, then sing another couple of praise songs.

Member

_____

Cell Leader

_____

We would like you to lead the **Offering** for this series, **Relationships based on the book of Ruth.**

This will be for _____   _____
(Insert dates)
_____ and _____

Remember that the offering is part of the worship, so allow it to flow easily from the time of worship.

Take a container for the offering – you could make one, or bring something that is precious to you.

Offering: Week 1

Before taking the offering, ask someone to give a testimony of how God has given to them because they have given faithfully to Him.

Offering: Week 2

Ask the group to spend a few moments speaking out some of the things God has given them, for example, homes, work, friends, parents, toys, health. Pray simply, thanking God for His goodness to us and thanking Him for accepting our offering as a token of our thanks.

Offering: Week 3

Spend a few moments asking everyone to share ways that they have seen God provide financially for the Church. Invite each person to pray and thank God after they have shared. Then take the offering.

Offering: Week 4

Ask someone to read Malachi 3:8-12 then ask, 'What do you think God is saying to us right now through these verses?'

Pray and pass around the offering container.

Member

_____

Cell Leader

_____

We would like you to lead the **Ministry** for this series, **Relationships, based on the book of Ruth.**

This will be for _____ _____
(Insert dates)

_____ and _____

Remember that the ministry will be part of the Word or the Witness section of the meeting. Keep the flow of the meeting as you move into ministry.

Ministry: Week 1

- The discussion on friendship may have opened up wounds in people who feel that they do not have friends, or who have been hurt by friends.
- Ask the group to get into groups of three and pray for each other about friends. Each person can share what they would like prayer for in the area of friendships.

Ministry: Week 2

- In pairs, read Romans 12:9-13 and then ask the Holy Spirit to speak to you. Share how you need to change to become a better friend.
- Pray together about this.
- We are to love God, love each other and love those who are lost to Jesus.

Ministry: Week 3

- Love God, love each other, love those who are lost to Jesus.
- Spend time letting the group move around and pray for different people – just a few minutes with each person. Pray that love flows between you all.

Ministry: Week 4

- No ministry.

Member

_____

Cell Leader

_____

We would like you to lead the **Witness** for this series, **Relationships, based on the book of Ruth.**

This will be for _____   _____
(Insert dates)
_____ and _____

This is about the witness of the group to those who do not know Jesus.

Pray and prepare before you go to the meeting. The devil will be totally opposed to souls being saved, but 'greater is He that is in you than he that is in the world'.

> ### Witness: Week 1
>
> - Stay in the small groups and share how you are getting on in friendships with people you are reaching out to. Each person write their friend's name on a piece of paper.
>
> - Bring the group back together and put all the names in the basket. Invite one adult and one child to pray over all the names in the basket.
>
> - Remind everyone that our commission is to 'love God, love each other and love those who are lost to Jesus'.

Witness: Week 2

- Pass round the basket with the names in and ask everyone to take out a name.
- Go round the group each praying just one sentence about the person whose name they drew out. It does not matter if the person praying does not know the name, or anything about the person named.
- Each find the person who originally wrote the name on the paper and add one need of that person to the paper, for example, a need for friends, for healing, for money.
- Agree in prayer for that need to be met, and see if there is anything that the group could do to meet that need in an appropriate way.
- Share as a whole group if there are needs that the whole group needs to address.
- Collect in the pieces of paper.

Witness: Week 3

- Lay all the pieces of paper with the names on the floor or a table in the centre.
- Invite each person to spend 30 seconds giving the rest of the group an update on their friend's situation.
- Ask everyone to pick up one piece of paper and pray for the person named on it for one minute. Repeat this, asking everyone to exchange papers. This can be repeated several times. It is fun and effective!

Witness: Week 4

- Spend some time letting people look at the sponsoring materials. Talk them through these and answer questions.
- Love God, love each other, love those who are lost to Jesus.

Series Five: Extracts from 1 Timothy

Background material for cell leader

Timothy's mother, Eunice, was a Jewish believer, but his father worshipped Greek gods (Acts 16:1). Timothy was well thought of in the place where he lived (Acts 16:2), which is a significant point. He travelled with Paul and became pastor to several churches. Paul wrote giving him help and advice with problems he was facing.

1 Timothy 1:17 is used as a concluding confession each week. Use the handout so everyone reads the same version (from the Youth Bible).

Beforehand

Before you begin this series, ask someone to prepare a creative overview of the story of Saul's conversion. This could be using pictures; acting it (using adults and children); rewriting it as a play and letting the whole group take part (remember that you need a crowd); a narration by a good story teller.

Themes and aims

In Worship, this series focuses on placing Jesus at the centre of everything, and creating a 'table of praise'.

In Word, we focus on parts of the book of Timothy, seeing the applications for ourselves today.

In Witness, we focus on prayer walking and planning an outreach event.

Kids' Slot material

The themes and aims of each series are the same as for those who are not in the Kid's Slot, as is the vision statement. Everyone takes part together in the Welcome section and the Worship. Rejoin the main group at the end of the Witness section to share and pray together before the meeting closes.

EXTRACTS FROM 1 TIMOTHY

Week 1

Preparation

This week you will need
- candle and matches
- an attractive container for the offering
- handout

Welcome

Icebreaker: If you could add one person to your family, who would it be and why?

Worship

- Place a candle in the centre of the group, then invite a child to light it, with the help of an older person if necessary.
- Ask someone to read John 8:12.
- Stand in a circle and reach out towards the candle, reminding the group that Jesus is here with us. He is at the centre of everything we do and everything we are.
- Sing a worship song several times.
- Ask a child to hold the candle as high as they safely can. Pray, thanking Jesus for being our light.
- Continue with another couple of worship songs, perhaps asking different children to stand in the middle holding the candle.

Offering

- Who can give one good reason why we should bring an offering when we meet together? Let several members give short answers.
- Pray, including some of the reasons in your prayer.
- Pass the offering container around.

Word *(personal application)*

This week is intended to challenge how we feel about people who join the cell, or people we meet who are completely opposed to us and our whole way of being. Do we have the heart of Jesus towards them?

- Show the story of Saul as previously prepared.
- Ask several people to read 1 Timothy 1:12-17, reminding them that this is Paul, who once killed Christians. Read 1 Timothy 1:12-17 again slowly.

- Ask two people from different age groups to read Acts 9:26.
- How did the Church feel about Paul? Scared, angry, fearful?
- Ask two more people from different age groups to read 1 Timothy 1:15-16.
- How did Jesus feel about Paul?
  - Jesus came for people like Paul (verse 15).
  - He did not judge Paul because He had taken his punishment (verse 15).
  - He was patient – 'without limit' (verse 16, Youth Bible).
  - He wanted Paul to give hope to others who were murderers, thieves, bullies, liars and the like (verse 16).
- When people like Paul come into our lives how will we feel? What will we do? Remember that what we feel often determines what we do!
- Who gets the glory and honour when someone like Paul becomes a Christian, and how does this happen? Do people see the change in their lives and know that no one but God could have done this?
- Finish by reading 1 Timothy 1:17 all together. You could read it again at the end of the meeting.

Ministry

In groups of three, spend a short time praying for each other, that our hearts will be ready to accept anyone Jesus sends to us. Children have problems with this, too, but are generally more accepting than adults. Remember Matthew 18:4.

Witness

Vision: Prayer walking is a powerful way to begin to take our neighbourhood for Jesus. It gives us the opportunity to 'walk the land' to see areas that need special prayer, and to have a greater insight into the area that we are reclaiming.

During this series, two or three people from different age groups will prayer walk the street where the cell meeting is being held. This will be for 10 minutes only. Always make sure one person has a watch, and the return time is made very clear.

The rest of the group start to plan a social outreach event.
- First of all, pray for the Holy Spirit to guide your plans.
- Look at the people you are reaching out to, and their interests. Is there something that everyone, or groups of these people, would enjoy?
- Do some like sport, art, gardening, theatre, cars, cookery? These activities may cross the age range, or they may be age-related. Either is fine.

- Ask someone to make a list and bring it to next week's meeting.
- It may be that you do not know the interests of some of the people you would like to invite, in which case ask people to try to find out and tell the cell at the next meeting.
- Give the people who have been prayer walking the opportunity to say how they got on, and then give them a brief outline of what the cell has done while they were out.

Finish   End the meeting by all standing and joining hands while someone prays, then say 1 Timothy 1:17 together, using the handout.

1 Timothy 1:17

To the King

who rules for ever,

who will never die,

who cannot be seen,

the only God,

be honour and glory

for ever and ever.

Amen.

EXTRACTS FROM 1 TIMOTHY

Kids' Slot material: Week 1

For the Witness part of this series, the children's co-ordinator needs to talk with the cell leader in the week before this meeting and decide whether the children are going to:
- plan their own social outreach event with adult support, in the same room as the rest of the cell
- plan their own social outreach event going through the same process as the rest of the cell but in a separate room

Each person taking the Kid's Slot this series needs to be aware of the decision made. If some or all of the children are going to remain separate, then the person taking the Kids Slot needs to be given the same witness material as the rest of the cell.

N.B. If your strategy involves having some children in the Kid's Slot and some remaining with the rest of the adults and youth, you will need to have them all together for the planning of this event.

Preparation

This week you will need
- a Bible that can be easily understood
- a couple of items of dressing-up clothes

Let all the children stay with everyone else to see/hear the story of Saul.

Begin by chatting together about the previous week, looking back at the previous week's cell meeting and talking through any follow-up, such as concerns they had, or things they were looking forward to. It is always good to relax and share together first, so building relationship with the children.

Word

Let the children experience the story again, perhaps letting some of them mime it as you read Acts 9:1-19.
- Invite one child to be Saul, putting on a relevant item of dressing up clothes. Ask them to leave the room and to come back in when you call out, 'Come in, Saul'. When the child comes back, ask the others to decide how they feel about him joining their cell.
- Read Acts 9:26 and show how the disciples felt when Saul came to join them.
- Invite another child, one everyone likes, to be Jesus and put on a relevant item of dressing-up clothes. Ask them to leave the room and to come back when you call out, 'Come in, Jesus'. When the child enters, ask the others to decide how they feel about him joining their cell.

- Read 1 Timothy 1:15 and talk together about Jesus' love for everyone, no matter what they have done or who they are.
- Talk about how Jesus would 'answer the door' to Saul. Then ask the person who was acting Saul to leave and enter again, and ask each child in turn to welcome him as Jesus would.
- Pray together and share any news from the previous week – share your news too!

Witness

- Let some of the children be involved with the prayer walk each week.
- Talk with your cell leader or children's co-ordinator about the process for planning and holding a social outreach for children.

Finish   End the meeting all together for the sharing and confession.

Week 2

Background information for cell leader

How is prophecy given?
- Prophecy can come in pictures or words. It may involve acting to demonstrate the truth that is being spoken.
- Prophecy is not usually telling someone specifically what to do, although it may involve promises for the future. It is not negative, destructive or condemning.

What is prophecy?
- It is a message from God that comes through a person.
- It can be anything, from one word or picture, to several pages, that someone believes God has given to them.
- It may be intended for the one who receives the message, for giving to someone else, for a group of people, or (if people are trusted by God) for a nation.

What is the aim of prophecy?
- Prophecy is intended for
  - edification: instructing or building people up
  - exhortation: encouraging people to do God's will
  - comfort: giving people a sense of well being and security knowing God is in charge, and knows what He is doing.

Preparation

This week you will need
- a note to give everyone reminding them to bring a praise token
- invitations to be completed in the Witness time
- copies of the background notes for this week

Welcome

Icebreaker: What is your favourite place in your home, and why is it special to you?

Worship

- Tell the group that next week we are going to make a 'table of praise', and ask each person to bring an item that reminds them of something special they can praise God for, for example a family photo, a souvenir from a special holiday, a wedding anniversary gift.
- Sing a couple of praise songs, repeating them as appropriate.
- Ask everyone to stand in a circle, and close their eyes. Jesus

WEEK 2

is here, He promised to be. He is standing right in the middle of us all. How is He looking as He looks at you? What is the expression on His face?
- Ask everyone to share, quietly, how they saw Him as He looked at them, and pray after sharing.
- Sing a couple of worship songs together.

Offering
- Ask if anyone has had a Scripture from God which has encouraged them to give. Give them a few moments to think about this, then ask one or two to share. Tell them that you will do the same next week.
- Ask the people who shared to pray before the offering is taken, then take the offering.

Word *(personal application)*

This week the focus is on prophecy, aiming to encourage those who have received prophecies but as yet they have not seen them fulfilled, and to release everyone into the gift of prophecy. Be sure that everyone understands that prophecy requires accountability.
- Ask several people to read 1 Timothy 1:18-19a.
- Ask if anyone can explain very simply what they think prophecy is.

    Prophecy can tell us the way to go, or where we are going to. After that we often encounter problems and difficulties in the way which tempt us to change direction. The prophetic word acts as a sword with which we can fight our way through until the prophecy is fulfilled.

    The group could act this out. One person receives a prophecy from another, then others come along to try to prevent him going forward, but he speaks out the prophecy each time until they give up and leave him.
- Ask if anyone has received a prophecy and seen it fulfilled. Then ask who has received a prophecy and not seen it happen yet.
- What things might try make us let go of the prophecies that have been given to us? The time it takes to happen? Having ideas of our own?
- What must we always do with prophecy? Check it out with a leader? Check it agrees with the Bible?
- Read 1 Timothy 1:18-19a again, leaving out 'Timothy, my son'.

Ministry Ask someone to be responsible for writing down any prophecy given, then letting the relevant person, or people, have a copy.

If you break into small groups for people to prophesy over each other, make sure a cell leader or responsible person is in each group. Remember to allow space for the children and younger Christians to give, as well as receive, words of prophecy.

Use this time for the Lord either to give a prophecy for the whole cell – write it down, ask some one to type it clearly and make sure everyone gets a copy; or to give a prophecy for individuals, starting with anyone who has never received one for themselves; or both could happen of course!

Witness

Vision: As we plan activities to which we can bring our unsaved friends, we all need to focus on those we will invite, and pray especially for them. Personal invitations bring personal responses, so each of us can reach out to another.

- Ask two or three different people, of different age groups if possible, to prayer walk the street where you are meeting. Check that one of them has a watch, and ask them to be no longer than 10 minutes.
- Look at the list of people you are reaching out to and find out if there is any new information about things they are especially interested in.
- Pray, inviting the Holy Spirit to guide your decisions.
- Fix a day, in three weeks' time, to invite these people to an event that will reflect their interests. Remember that this may be a whole group activity, or something for smaller groups that reflects their age, interest or venue. The key is that we are planning for others (although we will end up having a good time too!).
- Ask one person to be responsible for organising the details of each activity, giving the children some responsibility too.
- Hand out the invitations for everyone to fill in and take away.
- Pray in the groups in which you are going to have the activity. Pray for the people coming, for unity in the groups, for the practical details.

Finish Close the meeting by asking everyone to stand, join hands and pray, before saying 1 Timothy 1:17 together.
You may like to give out a copy of the background notes.

Kids' Slot material: Week 2

Preparation

This week you will need
- a Bible that is easy to understand
- materials for making invitations to the social outreach

Begin by chatting together about the previous week, looking back at the previous week's cell meeting and talking through any follow-up, such as concerns they had, or things they were looking forward to. It is always good to relax and share together first, so building relationship with the children.

Word

- Invite a child to read 1 Timothy 1:18.
- Tell the children about a prophecy you have received for your life, for the cell or the Church. Remember to make it interesting by telling them where it took place, who gave it and how people felt about it. Chat about it and make sure the children understand it.
- Ask a child to pretend to be Jesus and give this prophecy. Help them understand where prophecy comes from and that it is not just another promise.
- Ask the children if they know about any prophecies on their lives, or in any other situation, that they have seen come true. Then ask them to share any that they have not seen happen.
- Return to the rest of the cell for the ministry time and the prophetic spirit being released. Parents need to hear prophecy spoken over their children and children need to be released to prophesy over adults!

Witness

Continue with the same strategy as agreed with your cell leader and children's co-ordinator.

Finish

End the meeting by sharing and confessing 1 Timothy 1:17 together.

Week 3

Preparation

This week you will need
- small table and nice cloth for the table of praise
  N.B. The care you put into preparing the table will reflect to the group the importance you place on it.
- an attractive container for the offering

Welcome

Icebreaker: What was your happiest moment of this past week?

Worship

- Start with a song of praise, before praying.
- Ask each person to put the praise token they have chosen on the table of praise and explain to the group why they have chosen it.
- Tell everyone that you will be doing this again next week, and ask people to bring a different token.
- Go round the room, asking people to praise God for what He did for the person on their right.
- Give a clap offering!
- Sing a couple of praise songs.

Offering

Invite people to share scriptures that have encouraged them to give, then ask those who shared to pray about the offering before taking it.

Word *(personal application)*

This week you are identifying people in authority. Our attitudes and feelings towards them often cause us to de-personalise them and therefore not to pray for them as people whom Jesus loves, with needs of their own.

- Ask several people, from different age groups, to read 1 Timothy 2:1-4, 8.
- Ask someone to read verse 1 again.
- How do we pray for people? Do we pray for what they really need or do we just pray without thinking about that?
- How do we know what they need? For instance, by taking an interest in them, asking the Holy Spirit, asking them.
- Ask another person to read verse 2.

WEEK 3

- Who are 'those in authority' over you?
  N.B. verse 2 says if we pray for them, it will also benefit us!
- Ask everyone to get into groups of three or four. Then ask the following questions, allowing a few minutes for each one.
  - Name one person who is in authority over you, and who is not a Christian.
  - How do you feel when you are with them? People are often afraid of authority figures, and this stops them witnessing boldly for Jesus.
  - Have we really thought about the fact that Jesus wants them to know Him?
  - Do you know what their needs are?

Ministry

- Read I Timothy 1:8.
- Still in the small groups, pray particularly about negative feelings towards the people in authority. There may be a need to forgive them, and to repent for wrong attitudes towards them.
- Pray together for the person you have named in authority over you.

Witness

Vision: As we bring people to meetings or events with the cell group, we need to remember to spend time with those who are new to the group, taking an interest in them and being aware of areas of need they may have in order that we can reach into that need with the love of Jesus.

- Send two or three people from different age groups, who have not been before, out to prayer walk the street where you are meeting. Make sure one of them has a watch and knows to return in 10 minutes.
- Ask everyone to share how they got on giving out the invitations for the social outreach event.
- Divide into groups, according to the reactions the invitations received, for example, one group for those who met with negative attitude, one group for those invitations were accepted, one group for those who were refused. Pray that the Holy Spirit will show this group others to invite.
- Allow time for feedback from those who were prayer walking, and briefly tell them what the group has done.
- Ask people who were taking responsibility for the practical arrangements for the outreach event to give an update.

Finish

Close with everyone standing, holding hands, and praying together, before saying 1 Timothy 1:17 together.

EXTRACTS FROM 1 TIMOTHY

Kids' Slot material: Week 3

Preparation

This week you will need
- a Bible that is easy to understand
- paper
- pencils
- envelopes
- large sheet of paper
- marker pen

Begin by chatting together about the previous week, looking back at the previous week's cell meeting and talking through any follow-up, such as concerns they had, or things they were looking forward to. It is always good to relax and share together first, so building relationship with the children.

Word

- Brainstorm with the children about the people they recognise as being in authority over them, such as teachers, parents, cell leaders, police. Let them write or draw these on a large sheet of paper.
- Invite a child to read 1 Timothy 2:1-2, 8 and ask the children to share what they think these verses mean.
- Encourage the children to talk about what these people do to help them understand some of the difficulties they face in life.
- Now ask the children to choose one person who is in authority over them. Ask them to share how they feel about that person, and, if they are ready, let them repent of any wrong attitudes towards them.
- Invite a child to read 1 Timothy 2:1-2, 8 again.
- Let each child write a thank you letter, or draw a picture, to send to a local 'authority', for example the school, the local police, the fire brigade. Let them put the letters in an envelope. Post the letters yourself, or if possible, let the children go with you and pray outside the place where you will deliver them.

Witness

Continue with the same strategy as agreed with your cell leader and children's co-ordinator.

Finish

End the meeting by sharing and confessing 1 Timothy 1:17 together.

Week 4

Preparation

This week you will need
- small table and an attractive cloth to go on it, remembering that the care you take in setting it up will reflect the importance you place on the table
- an attractive container for the offering

Welcome

Icebreaker: What does, or did, God mean to you as a child?

Worship

- Sing a song of praise.
- Let everyone who has brought a praise token, put it on the table of praise and say why they have brought it.
- Give a clap offering to Jesus.
- Ask each person in turn to go to the table, pick up something on it that they did not bring, and thank Jesus for what it represents.
- Sing another couple of praise songs.

Offering

- Focus on the fact that Jesus has given us so much, and we give Him a token of our thanks as we bring our offering to Him.
- Pray and pass around the offering container.

Word *(personal application)*

This week the emphasis is on letting the children be heard, and allowing the group to understand how they are feeling as part of the cell. If there are no children in the cell, the group can look at the benefits of having children, and see how they experience these in their own lives. Finally there is the opportunity to look at particular aspects of the children's lives.

- Invite several people, from different age groups, each to read 1 Timothy 4:12.
- Ask an adult to read verse 12a, then either if you have children or young people in your group, ask them how they feel in the group.
  - Do they feel important?
  - How do they know that they are really needed and wanted?
  - Is there anything more the cell can do to help them?

EXTRACTS FROM 1 TIMOTHY

– What is the best thing about the cell?
– What is the worst thing about the cell?

How honest the children's replies are will depend on the level of trust and acceptance in the group. Explore their feelings, and encourage the group to really 'hear' and respond to them, making adjustments as appropriate; for instance, if desirable it is acceptable and proper to apologise to a child. Or if there are no children or young people in the cell, explore the concept.

– How important do you feel the children and young people are?
– How would you feel if there were some in our cell?
– What evidence is there in your life that children and young people are important?

- Ask someone to read verse 12b.
- Our words, our actions, our love, our faith, and the purity of our lives are really important. They are important to us and to others who are watching us as Jesus' family on this earth.
- Break into groups of three or four, take two of these areas, and discuss how you get on in them. Age-related groups might be a good idea this time, so for example, children look at words and actions – youth look at love and purity of life – adults look at words and faith.

Ministry   Stay in the small groups and pray into the areas where people are having difficulties.

Witness

Vision: Ask one or two new members of the cell to share why they joined and what it has been like to be a member of the cell. This can be a very revealing time, when all members can learn how to welcome people into their cell more effectively.

- Ask two or three people of different age groups to prayer walk the street where you are meeting. Make sure one person has a watch, and confirm that they should return in 10 minutes.
- Ask the people responsible for organising the social outreach events to confirm details.
- Break into the groups that will be meeting together for the outreach and pray for every person who will be attending, group members, and non-Christians alike.
- Ask the people who have been prayer walking to say how they got on and briefly tell them what the group has been doing.

Finish   Close by standing in a circle, holding hands, and saying 1 Timothy 1:17 together.

Kids' Slot material: Week 4

Preparation

This week you will need
- a Bible that is easy to understand

This week the group needs to be all together, but the person taking the Kid's Slot could focus on the children and help if there are any problems.

Witness

Continue with the same strategy as agreed with your cell leader and children's co-ordinator.

Finish

End the meeting by sharing and confessing 1 Timothy 1:17 together.

Delegation forms

Series Five: Extracts from 1 Timothy

Member

_____

Cell Leader

_____

We would like you to do the **Icebreaker** for this series, **Extracts from 1 Timothy.**

This will be for _____ _____
(Insert dates)
_____ and _____

Remember that you tell the group what the question is, then answer it yourself before passing it around and giving each person a chance to answer. If anyone has trouble thinking of their answer, come back to them later.

Icebreaker: Week 1

If you could add one person to your family, who would it be and why?

Icebreaker: Week 2

What is your favourite place in your home and why is it special to you?

Icebreaker: Week 3

What was one of the happiest moments of this past week?

Icebreaker: Week 4

What does, or did, God mean to you as a child?

Member
_____

Cell Leader
_____

We would like you to lead the **Worship** for this series, **Extracts from 1 Timothy**.

This will be for _____   _____
(Insert dates)
_____ and _____

This should last approximately ___ minutes. Songs will need to be easily repeated. If necessary you could have sheets for everyone to use (you could write these and photocopy them). You may like to use tapes that you have pre-recorded, so that songs are in the right sequence. Alternatively you could ask someone to play a guitar (or other instrument), or sing unaccompanied. Be creative – God is a very creative God – just look at the universe!

The following are outlines for the worship time; however you will need to create a flow and invite the Holy Spirit into this framework.

Worship: Week 1

- Place a candle in the centre of the group, then ask a child to light it, with the help of an older person if necessary.
- Ask someone to read John 8:12
- Stand in a circle and reach out to the candle, reminding the group that Jesus is here with us. He is at the centre of everything we do and everything we are.
- Sing a worship song several times.
- Ask a child to hold the candle as high as they safely can, then pray, thanking Jesus for being our light.
- Continue with another couple of worship songs, perhaps asking different children to stand in the middle holding the candle while this is done.

Worship: Week 2

- Tell the group that next week we are going to make 'a table of praise', and ask each person to bring an item that reminds them of something special they can praise God for, such as a family photo, a souvenir from a special holiday, a wedding anniversary gift.

- Sing a couple of praise songs, repeating them as appropriate.

- Ask everyone to stand in a circle, and close their eyes. Remind them that Jesus is here, He promised to be. He is standing right in the middle of us all. Ask them, how is He looking as He looks at them?

- Ask everyone to share, quietly, how they saw Him as He looked at them, and pray after sharing.

Sing a couple of worship songs together.

Worship: Week 3

- Start with a song of praise, before praying.

- Ask each person to put the item that they have chosen on the table, and to explain to everyone why they have chosen it.

- Tell everyone that you will be doing this again next week, and ask people to bring something different.

- Go round the room and ask people to praise God for what He has done for the person on their right.

- Give a clap offering!

- Sing a couple of praise songs.

Worship: Week 4

- Sing a song of praise

- Let everyone who has brought something for the table of praise put it on the table, and say why they have bought it.

- Give a clap offering to Jesus.

- Ask each person in turn to go to the table, pick up something on it that they did not bring, and thank Jesus for what it represents.

- Sing another couple of praise songs.

Member

_____

Cell Leader

_____

We would like you to lead the **Offering** for this series, **Extracts from 1 Timothy**.

This will be for _____   _____
(Insert dates)
_____ and _____

Remember that the offering is part of the worship, so allow it to flow easily from the time of worship.

Take a container for the offering – you could make one, or bring something that is precious to you.

Offering: Week 1

- Who can give one good reason why we should bring an offering when we meet together? Let several members give short answers.
- Pray, including some of the reasons that have been given.
- Pass the offering container around.

Offering: Week 2

- Ask who has a Scripture that God has given them which has encouraged them to give. Give them a few moments to think about this, then ask one or two to share.
- Tell them that you will do the same next week.
- Ask the people who shared to pray before the offering is taken.

Offering: Week 3

- Ask people to share Scriptures that have encouraged them to give, then ask those who shared to pray about the offering before taking it.

Offering: Week 4

- Focus on the fact that Jesus has given us so much, and we give Him a token of our thanks as we bring our offering to Him. Pray before taking the offering.

Member
_____

Cell Leader

_____

We would like you to lead the **Ministry** for this series, **Extracts from 1 Timothy**.

This will be for _____   _____
(Insert dates)
_____ and _____

Remember that the ministry will be part of the Word or the Witness section of the meeting. Keep the flow of the meeting as you move into ministry.

Ministry: Week 1

- In groups of three, spend a short time praying for each other, that our hearts will be ready to accept anyone Jesus sends to us. Children have problems with this, too, but are generally more accepting than adults.

- Remember Matthew 18:4.

Ministry: Week 2

- Ask someone to be responsible for writing down any prophecy given, then letting the relevant person, or people, have a copy. Break into small groups for people to prophesy over each other, making sure a cell leader or responsible person is in each group.

- Remember to allow space for the children and younger Christians to give, as well as receive, words of prophecy.

- Use this time for the Lord either to give a prophecy for the whole cell (write it down, ask someone to type it clearly and make sure everyone gets a copy) or to give a prophecy for individuals, starting with anyone who has never received one for themselves. (Or both could happen of course!)

Ministry: Week 3

- Read 1 Timothy 1:8.

- Still in the small groups, pray particularly about negative feelings towards the people in authority. There may be a need to forgive them, and to repent for wrong attitudes towards them.

- Pray together for the person you have named in authority over you.

Ministry: Week 4

- Stay in the small groups and pray into the areas where people are having difficulties.

Member

_____

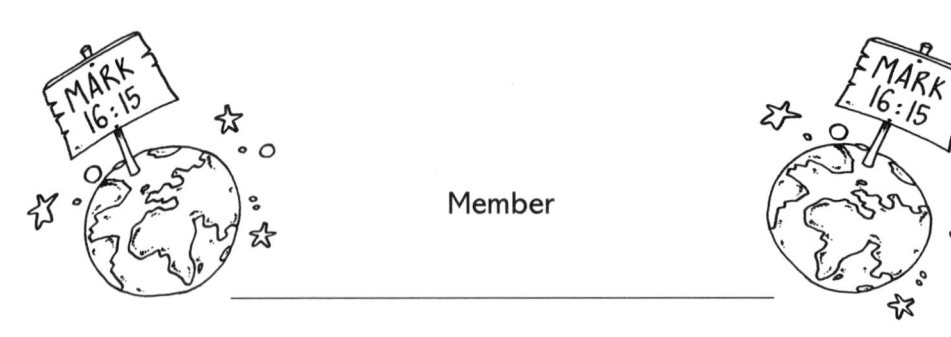

Cell Leader

_____

We would like you to lead the **Witness** for this series, **Extracts from 1 Timothy**.

This will be for _____   _____
(Insert dates)
_____ and _____

This is about the witness of the group to those who do not know Jesus.

Pray and prepare before you go to the meeting. The devil will be totally opposed to souls being saved, but 'greater is He that is in you than he that is in the world'.

Witness: Week 1

- For this series two or three people, from different age groups, will prayer walk the street where the cell meeting is being held. This will be for 10 minutes only. Always make sure one person has a watch, and the return time is made very clear.

- The rest of the group start to plan a 'social outreach' event. Begin by praying for the Holy Spirit to guide your plans.

- Look at the people you are reaching out to, and their interests. Is there something that everyone, or groups of these people, would enjoy? Do some like sport, art, gardening, theatre, cars, cookery? These activities may cross the ages, or they may be age related (either is fine). Ask someone to make a list and bring that list again next week.

- It may be that you do not know the interests of some of the people you would like to invite. Ask people to try to find out and tell the cell at the next meeting.

- Give the people who have been prayer walking the opportunity to say how they got on, and then give them a brief outline of what the cell has done while they were out.

Witness: Week 2

- Ask two or three different people, using different age groups if possible, to prayer walk the street where you are meeting. Check that one of them has a watch, and ask them to be no longer than 10 minutes.

- Look at the list of people you are reaching out to and check if there is any new information about things they are especially interested in.

- Pray, inviting the Holy Spirit to guide your decisions.

- Fix a day, in three weeks time, when you can invite these people to something that will reflect their interests. Remember that this may be a whole group activity, or something for smaller groups that reflects their age, interest or venue. The key is that we are planning for others – although we will end up having a good time too!

- Ask one person to responsible for organising the details of each activity, giving children some responsibility too.

- Hand out the invitations for everyone to fill in and take away.

- Pray in the groups in which you are going to have the activity. Pray for the people coming, for unity in the groups, for the practical details.

Witness: Week 3

- Send two or three people, from different age groups, who have not been out yet, to prayer walk the street where you are meeting. Make sure one of them has a watch and knows to return in 10 minutes. Ask everyone to share how they got on giving out the invitations for the social outreach event.

- Divide into groups, according to the reactions the invitations received, for example, one group for those who met with negative attitudes, one group for those whose invitations were accepted, one group for those who were refused. Pray that the Holy Spirit will show this group others to invite.

- Allow time for feedback from those who were prayer walking, and briefly tell them what the group has done.

- Ask people who were taking responsibility for the practical arrangements for the outreach event to give an update.

Witness: Week 4

- Ask two or three people, of different age groups, to prayer walk the street where you are meeting. Make sure one person has a watch, and confirm that they should return in 10 minutes.

- Ask the people responsible for organising the social outreach events to confirm details.

- Break into the groups that will be meeting together for the outreach and pray for every person who will be attending (group members and non-Christians).

- Ask the people who have been prayer walking to say how they got on and briefly tell them what the group has been doing.

Appendix 1: Seminars

These seminars are for you if you can identify with any of the following:
- Have you wondered how to integrate your children and young people totally into the body of Christ?
- Are you lacking the resources and training and therefore unsure of the way forward?
- Do you wonder how your church can have one vision and move together, adults, young people and children?
- Do you want your whole church to grow, learn and experience kingdom life in the way God intended . . . together?
- Are you Cell Church and wanting to integrate the children?

Important points with regard to seminars:

(a) The seminars are visionary with a strong biblical foundation as well as very practical, with their emphasis being on the outworking of the vision in the local church.

(b) It is essential for the senior leadership to attend the seminar in order to carry the vision to their own congregation. However, the format is kept simple so that anyone can participate and lead intergenerational groups.

(c) Seminars vary between one and three days, depending on the number of workshops held. Obviously the longer the seminar, the more practical experience and personal application can be incorporated. Churches usually have seminars for Friday evening and all day Saturday.

(d) Seminars include discussion of, and where possible some experience of, the intergenerational celebration and corporate prayer life of the church. Leaders of worship, celebration and prayer meetings are strongly encouraged to attend.

(e) A manual will be used so that leaders can replicate the seminar with their own church. However, the more people from your church who attend the seminar, the clearer will be the vision and the greater the anointing taken back.

If you are considering being an intergenerational church or having intergenerational cells and would like to host or attend one of Daphne Kirk's seminars contact her at:

The Lighthouse Centre
13 Lynn Road, Ely, Cambs CB7 4EG

Telephone: 01353 662228   Fax: 01353 662179
E-mail: ecf@lhouse.win-uk.net

Appendix 2: Other intergenerational cell materials from Daphne Kirk

Heirs Together
Establishing intergenerational Cell Church

Hand in Hand
Sponsoring a child using *Living with Jesus – an equipping track for children*

When a child asks to be baptised

Living with Jesus – an equipping track for children
Book 1: Welcome to God's family
Book:2: Special times and gifts
Book 3: Talking and listening
Book 4: Love for me and ,ove for others
Book 5: Strongholds
Book 6: What do we choose?
Book 7: Having faith
Book 8: Fighting together

All published by Kevin Mayhew Publishers.

Appendix 3: Useful forms . . .

. . . for ideas,
to photocopy,
or just to browse through!

APPENDIX 3

Cell Meeting for _____ (date)
To be prayed over by you and the leadership team.

Cell Leaders _____

Cell Leaders (*in training*) _____

Meeting started at _____ and ended at _____

Members absent	Reason for absence

New attenders	Notes

General report of the meeting
(Overall spirit, most significant events, weaknesses or problems)

Interaction during the week (past and present)
Pastoral, members (is it inclusive or cliquish), etc.

Sponsoring and accountability
Please list people being sponsored and who by. Then give a brief report on progress.

Please list accountability partners and give brief report on progress.

If you have most of your group involved, please list them a few each week.

Youth
Are they participating, problems, encouragements.

Have you asked about and prayed for their youth cells?

APPENDIX 3

Children *Name of person responsible this series* _____
(Are they participating/any problems/are they having interaction with members between meetings?)

Have you asked about, and prayed for your children's cell meeting?

Prayer meetings *Name of person responsible this series* _____

Dates _____ Venues _____

_____   _____

Total Number: adults _____ secondary school _____

                                   primary school _____

Worship *Name of person responsible for this series* _____

Ministry *Name of person responsible for this series* _____

Word (personal application)

Please state if anyone other than the Cell Leader took this

Any comments on this series in particular?

Witness (Works) and evangelism in the group generally

Names of people responsible for this series _____

Please be specific about plans for and reports on group evangelism, social outreach events and personal evangelism, etc.

How are you?

Is there anything you would particularly like help for? Are you all right? Any personal encouragements, etc?

APPENDIX 3

Adults/Youth: For the next few weeks the Word (personal application) in your cell groups will be sharing about how the sermon impacted you. If you would like to make some notes this may help you to share more fully!

Children: Take this sheet to your cell group this week so you can talk about some of the things said in the sermon that were really important to you. You may use writing or drawings, whichever you like!

APPENDIX 3

Cell Meeting Attendance Record

(It is recommended that this be filled in by the co-ordinator
using the Meeting Evaluation Form)

Series commencing _____ and ending _____

Please list married couples and all children individually

Weeks

Name	1	2	3	4	5	6

Member's Information

Name _____ Date of birth _____

Address _____

_____

_____

Tel no: _____

Marital status _____

Occupation _____ Work tel no: _____

Driver Yes/No _____ Car owner Yes/No _____

Children	D.O.B.	School	Cell

Cell Leader _____ Date _____

Cell Leader _____ Date _____

Cell Leader _____ Date _____

APPENDIX 3

Member's Information (Youth/Children)

Name _____ Date of birth _____

Address _____

_____

_____

Tel no: _____

School/college _____

Do parents attend a cell? (please specify) _____

Are parents/carers 'born again'? _____

Parents'/carers' names _____

Relationships _____

Brothers/sisters (name and age) _____

_____

Do they attend a cell? _____

Cell Leader _____ Date _____

Cell Leader _____ Date _____

Cell Leader _____ Date _____

Cell Leader _____ Date _____

Hosting Schedule

Cell Leaders _____

Co-ordinator _____

Meeting night this series _____

Person responsible for hosting schedule _____

Number of copies required from the office _____

Date	Name	Address	Phone no.

APPENDIX 3

Cell responsibilities for this series

The Cell Leader remains responsible for Word (personal aplication), evaluation forms, pastoral strategy, sponsoring/accountability.

Hosting schedule (put in file for copying) _____

Prayer chain (put in file for copying) _____

Cell prayer meetings (arrange weekly) _____

Birthdays (see Cell Leader) _____

Transport (arrange as necessary) _____

Ushering (remind cell and head up) _____

Notices (collect from Cell Leader) _____

Icebreaker _____

Worship (15 minutes, be creative) _____

Offering (bring an attractive container) _____

Ministry (15 minutes) _____

Witness (15 minutes) _____

Children's co-ordinator
(check children included and all right) _____

Social interaction (check all included,
arrange social event) _____

Evangelism (individual and group outreach) _____

Anything else! _____

Any member unable to fulfil their responsibility any particular week should find a substitute themselves and notify _____

Prayer and Communication Chain

Cell Leader(s) _____

Names should be entered as families, families pray together!

(Please phone the person whose name appears after yours on the prayer chain.)

Name _____ Phone no. _____

Name _____ Phone no. _____

Name _____ Phone no. _____

Name _____ Phone no. _____

Name _____ Phone no. _____

Name _____ Phone no. _____

Name _____ Phone no. _____

Name _____ Phone no. _____

Name _____ Phone no. _____

Name _____ Phone no. _____

Name _____ Phone no. _____

Last person phones the person at the top of the list!

If you are unable to contact the person under your name, ring the next available person, and keep trying to contact the person who was unavailable.